spliffs2

FURTHER ADVENTURES IN CANNABIS CULTURE

spliffs2

FURTHER ADVENTURES IN CANNABIS CULTURE

QUICK AMERICAN

Spliffs 2: Further Adventures in Cannabis Culture

Published by Quick American
A division of Quick Trading Company
Oakland, California
ISBN: 0-932551-72-6
         978-0932-55172-6

First published in Great Britain in 2004 by Collins & Brown
An Imprint of Chrysalis Books Group Plc

Text © Tim Pilcher
Volume © Chrysalis Books Group Plc 2004

Commissioning editor: Chris Stone
Editor: Ian Kearey
Designer: Philip Clucas MSIAD
Color reproduction: Anorax
Printed in China
Additional text by Rob Tribe and Michelle Guilford

The Publishers would like to thank

Library of Congress Cataloging-in-Publication Data available on file.

Contents

Introduction

**When I started this book I was a bit apprehensive.
I mean sequels are generally crap. What can be said
in a sequel that hasn't been covered previously? Well,
in the case of cannabis, a hell of a lot.**

Marijuana, like all important things in life, doesn't exist in a vacuum. Laws are constantly being changed, new ways of getting high are invented and legalization campaigns gain credence. The world turns, events evolve and so there is a need to maintain a foot in the past while keeping an eye on the future. But where to begin? There is so much information, all of it equally valid and important, that it became a mind-boggling challenge.

Ultimately, there was too much information to fit it into a book this size. So you won't discover that, unsurprisingly, marijuana is still officially the world's most popular drug, according to the United Nations Office on Drugs and Crime's (UNODC) 2002 report. You won't find out that

of the 200 million people who smoke, snort or pop pills, 163 million of them prefer cannabis. Compared with 34 million on amphetamines, 15 million doing opiates, 14 million snorting cocaine and a mere eight million dropping ecstasy the sacred herb wins easily. And it's getting more popular. Two-thirds of the 86 countries in the report believed that cannabis consumption and production had increased in 2001 and overall seizures of cannabis (the only way 'The Man' has of checking his facts) rose by 40 per cent between 1998 and 2001.

Nowhere in this book are tales about Sri Lanka's 200,000 tokers and the government's destruction of 300 tonnes of illegally cultivated cannabis in 1994. You definitely won't find anything about the former cannabis growers in Northern Bangladesh, now demanding government compensation for losses caused by the relatively new prohibition, instated in 1984.

Nor will you read about Veronica Mouser, a 13-year-old Californian schoolgirl (a non-smoker) whose project about the medicinal uses of marijuana was banned from a display in her school.

Mouser's project, *Mary Jane for Pain*, took months of work. 'This is a controversial subject and it should be discussed,' she said. Veronica interviewed doctors and studied three medical marijuana patients, but in a typically repressive US school move head teacher Deborah Ferguson said projects are supposed to be hands-on and marijuana is still an illegal drug. 'I think they just didn't like what I had to say, or talking about it, so they block it out and that's not science,' retorted the switched-on teenager.

What you will find is how sensimilla has influenced, inspired and ignited music – in particular rap – stand-up comedy and some of the most radical free thinkers on the planet in the Top 50 Greatest Potheads chapter. You'll also find recipes for the craziest cannabis cocktails – for reference only! – and not forgetting the spotter's guide to the most incredible pot paraphernalia ever made. There is a travelogue with advice on getting stoned around the world, along with one of the most detailed guides to growing grass available in regular bookshops. Plus, features on Kama Sutra while smoking weed, hemp clothing and that perennial problem, What to do when you're too stoned.

The first *Spliffs* book is a fantastic journey detailing the magical history of marijuana and its deep roots. *Spliffs 2* has nurtured those delicate seedling ideas and grown them under the 1,000-watt bulbs of the present. Who knows, maybe a *Spliffs 3* will reap the rich harvest of the end of cannabis prohibition in the future. But for now, here's hoping this sequel helps the cause and is more *Aliens* than *Jaws 4*.

Tim Pilcher, Brighton, June 2004

Chapter 1

The Plant

There isn't a single plant on the planet that has been as successful as cannabis. It grows in practically every corner of the globe and has endless uses that are still being discovered. Yet for all its plaudits and praise, it is also the most vilified and reviled shrub, demonized as 'killer weed'. But what's the truth behind the terror of this little green bush?

The Plant

Cannabis, or hemp, has grown wild across the planet since before man, and has been cultivated since the dawn of the earliest civilizations. Hemp's varied uses are almost without limit. It is possibly the most versatile and useful plant in existence.

Handy Hemp

Originally it was used for livestock feed, and to a lesser extent food for humans. Hemp seed's proteins resemble proteins in human blood, making them easier to digest, and they contain essential fatty acids with almost no saturated fat. Just one handful of seeds, eaten daily, will provide the adequate dose of proteins and essential oils an adult human needs.

When cannabis seeds are crushed they secrete an oil very similar to linseed oil, and this was used to make paints and varnishes until petrochemicals were introduced in the late 1930s. Hemp seed oil was also the world's principal source of combustible oil for lamps until the early 1800s, when it was overtaken by whale oil and then by kerosene in the late 1850s.

The plant can also be used for weaving textiles and was heavily used in the construction of ships' canvas sails, sealant, rope, rugs, carpets and drapes. Hemp was also one of the first plants to be used for making paper, and is far more economical than wood, as one acre of hemp could be used to make the same amount of paper as four acres of trees. Until it was generally outlawed around the globe in the first half of the 20th century, the hemp industry was responsible for the vast majority of paper and

Above: Giving the term 'greenhouse' new meaning, cannabis thrives under glass.

cloth in the world, with 80 per cent coming from Russia between 1740 and 1940.

Desperate not to become a slave to large oil corporations, car manufacturer Henry Ford realized that fossil fuels could be replaced by a renewable fuel source, like hemp, which can be converted to make methane, methanol or petrol (gasoline) at a fraction of the cost using coal, oil or natural gas. In 1941 Ford even constructed a working automobile entirely from hemp compounds, which was strong enough to withstand a blow from a crowbar.

Putting a Name to the Plant

Swedish botanist Carolus Linnaeus first classified the wild weed as *Cannabis sativa* in 1753 while in the Himalayan foothills of India. He believed it was the sole specimen of the genus, a monotypic species. However, in the East Indies in 1785 Jean Baptiste de Lamarck, a French biologist, discovered and named a second species, *Cannabis indica*. It wasn't for another 139 years that a third type was discovered. In 1924 the botanist D.E. Janischevsky categorized the least-known, *Cannabis ruderalis*, in southeast Russia.

C. sativa grows very tall and loosely branched, whereas *C. indica* is smaller, more conical or pyramidal in shape, and has denser branches. *C. ruderalis* is also small, but has less branches. Of the three, *C. indica* tends to have the highest psychoactive content and so is the most popular for smoking; however, there are many strains that now exist that have been cross-bred between

11

C. indica and *C. sativa. C. ruderalis* has little or no active ingredients, so it's usually used for making cloth, paper and so on, and has had the moniker 'industrial hemp' stuck to it.

The cannabis plant is a hardy annual that requires little space, grows well almost anywhere and requires no pesticides, as stoner band the Happy Mondays' ex-dancer Bez bitterly attested in his book, *Freaky Dancin'*. He was pulled over by Manchester's CID with four 'puny seedlings' in the boot of his car. They were 'the result of a stoned experiment that I'd abandoned… now I was being hailed as the Percy fuckin' Thrower of cannabis. I hate gardenin', I hate tendin' plants – why hadn't they shrivelled up with neglect, like every other plant I owned?'

Above (left to right): Cannabis comes in many shapes and colours; the classic Afghan, Double Dutch and Blueberry. Opposite page: Growing wild.

Marijuana's roots reach deep into the soil, and growing plants in the same soil for 20 years has shown little or no depreciation in the soil quality, unlike, for example, peanuts, which can completely destroy a soil's nutrient content if over-farmed. As cannabis leaves fall – assuming someone hasn't smoked them first – and decompose on the soil, they return essential nitrogen and minerals, which are beneficial for the soil and plant. Even the process of treating the stalks and branches of the plant, to prepare it

Freaky Fashions

If you smoke it, wear it. Hemp clothing is the fashion accessory for the serious toker. It's time to ditch the beads and beards and wear your weed upon your sleeve.

Of course industrial hemp doesn't contain enough THC to get you high (0.3% as opposed to the 3–10% in good grass), so don't even think of smoking your T-shirt when your stash runs dry. Even so, *Cannabis ruderalis*' relationship with its smokable sisters is close enough for production to have been banned in America in 1937, despite a brief flirtation with growing hemp during World War II for the war effort. The ban soon spread to the rest of the world and effectively sent a very reliable and profitable fabric industry off the rails.

As long ago as 450BC the Scythians and Thracians made hemp linens and, owing to its strength and weatherproof qualities, hemp was widely used in Europe and America for uniforms and work clothes, up until the mid-19th century

when the more soil pernicious cotton took over. In the late 1890s clothing companies started using re-cycled hemp sail cloth, and as Nimes, France, was the only place where the blue dye could be sourced, the fabric of the late 20th century was born and christened denim. Levi Strauss's original jeans, those American icons, were originally made from hemp and the company is now planning to re-introduce the idea. Italian fashion god Giorgio Armani is already there with hemp jeans in his collections and he celebrated the fabric back in 1996, 'Hemp produces a strong, clean yarn, with a structure that makes the cloth cool in summer and warm and comfortable in winter.' The other big boys of fashion Ralph Lauren and Calvin Klein are also increasing the use of hemp in their

Left: Hemp's diversity means it can be used for rough string and rope to fine, cotton-like T-shirts and all points between.

successfully combine environmental considerations with a radical fashion statement. Similar in appearance to linen, hemp makes stylish shirts, jackets and suits not to mention sturdy jeans, bags, shoes and belts. US designer Lisa

lines, although their motivation may well be pocket rather than planet – 'It's going to be a gigantic market,' enthused Owen Sercus, professor at the Fashion Institute of New York, in 1995.

China and Romania are two of the most important producers of hemp for clothing while German hemp is reputed to be some of the finest and softest wear around. 'Hemp is now regarded as the eco-friendly fibre,' according to Lynda Brown in her book *Organic Living*. The wonderful weed is used to make beautiful clothes that

Sauvageau sings hemp's aesthetic praise, 'I am not going to use hemp just because it is hemp. I chose it because of the texture. It's right for what I do. It has a very linen-like finish and the speckles are very beautiful.'

But surely the reason to wear hemp is because it is hemp. It's a statement. It's the ultimate eco-fabric, it's biodegradable, softer, stronger and more durable than cotton, it keeps you both warm and cool and when it's well processed and creatively put together, it's gorgeous too.

Above: Pharmaceutical cannabis is grown under secure conditions in the UK.

for pulping, returns essential nutrients to the earth, instead of using harmful chemicals that pollute the land.

Sensimilla Science

Cannabis is dioecious, meaning it comes as separate male and female plants, and it's the latter that produces the sweet resin beloved of smokers. It's important to separate the sexes as early as possible in order to get the best harvest. The male plants are taller, skinnier and have flower-like pods which contain the fertilizing, pollen-generating anthers. The female plant is darker, shorter and generally more squat, and also has short hairs protruding at the end of bracteole pods.

Cannabis is the only plant to contain the chemical elements known as cannabinoids. Almost 40 cannabinoids have been discovered and isolated so far, but only six of them are psychoactive. The most well-known is Delta 9-Tetrahydrocannabinol ($C_{21}H_{30}O_2$). All cannabis contains at least some Delta 9-THC, although industrial hemp contains only minute traces. Most cannabis grown for recreational use contains much more, with some plants made up of 25 per cent Delta 9-THC.

Left and above: Busted! The police, the thorn in the side of any potential herbal horticulturalist, seize UK crops.

The second psychoactive cannabinoid is Delta 9-THC's weaker cousin, Delta 8-THC, which is usually present in very low concentrations, and so the majority of herbal horticulturists and researchers ignore this compound and concentrate on the more potent Delta 9-THC.

Cannabidiol, also known as CBD, appears in nearly all forms of cannabis in varying degrees. CBD is the compound found to give the sedative effect to the high experience. CBD has the tendency to delay, but also prolong, the high. Whether CBD increases or decreases the strength of the high, depends on the individual smoker's tolerance.

17

Cannabinol, or CBN, is produced as THC oxidizes or degrades. Only trace amounts appear in fresh buds, but stored or cured (dried) buds and hashish tend to have higher amounts of CBN because the THC has degraded in the preparation process. Research has revealed that CBN gives a smoker a disoriented or sleepy effect, known as a 'stupefying high'. At best, CBN contains only 10 per cent of the psychoactive effect of the original Delta 9-THC.

The compound associated with the fragrance of the plant is THCV, or Tetrahydrocannabivarin. Very pungent-smelling cannabis, such as Skunk, usually contains high amounts of THCV, and it's also found in very potent marijuana originating from Southeast and Central Asia and Africa. These high concentrations of THCV will make the high come on quicker, but last shorter.

Cannabichromene, or CBC, makes up to 20 per cent of the cannabinoid compound of the cannabis plant. Although little research has been done, scientists and professional growers think that CBC might interact with THC to make for a more intense high.

Armed with all this knowledge, home-grown horticulturists have taken to splicing, cross-pollinating and nurturing a vast variety of strains in order to get the precise high they are looking for. Many breeders now concentrate on developing stronger psychoactive compounds in the plant by controlling the growth process. This is done in a variety of ways using lamps and bulbs, ventilation and soil nutrients, hydroponics, rock-wool, salt-free sand, etc. This can make ganja gardening an expensive, but ultimately satisfying, hobby.

While illegal in the US, in the UK the sale and ownership of hemp seeds is legal. The only way to break the law is when a gardener starts to germinate the seeds. However, this hasn't stopped anybody, and in 1997 it was estimated that just over a third (35 per cent) of all weed smoked in the UK was home-grown.

Growing cannabis is a relatively simple task. It's a hardy annual plant that survives well in temperate climates and can be grown in or outdoors in basic soil. In fact it thrives so well in the natural climate of the UK that the local council at Glastonbury, home of the legendary rock festival, have given up cutting down the wild-growing cannabis, sowed there by magnanimous marijuana-smoking festi-goers. And apparently there are plants just outside Manchester that are 'just over three metres high, seven metres round and have produced twenty-six ounces [730g] of Skunk Number One,' according to one breeder. However, to really get the best from the seeds, like any gardening, 'It takes years to get really good at it. There are unbelievable amounts of information to learn,' one Canadian grower warned.

The Need for Seed

Cannabis seed selection can be like choosing a fine wine. Plants are picked for their citrus aromas, their blueberry taste, or simply for the

Above: Holland's legendary grow shop, Positronics, launched their Nirvana seed bank in 1995, selling controversial feminized seeds.

With so many new breeders and seed companies coming into the market in recent years, cannabis seeds are a minefield of discussion these days. It's possible to buy seeds on the Internet from top cannabis breeders and reputable companies from all over the world, including Switzerland, Canada and South Africa. These days the best tend to come from Dutch companies, such as Ben Dronkers' Sensi Seed Bank, and Serious Seeds. Many have a high germination success rate, as they are kept in cannabis-seed storage units which keep them fresh and prevent them from drying out.

The safest and most reliable seeds are top-quality F1 hybrid strains. These are stabilized seeds that have been selectively inbred over several generations so that the desired traits are guaranteed. This process can take up to four years, using a staggering 20,000 plants, but the end result is always worth it. However, there are still companies that sell unstabilized strains (hybrids from hybrids), which have unpredictable results.

A relatively new development in seed technology is 'feminized seeds'. These are seeds that are allegedly guaranteed only to sprout female flowers, avoiding the hassle of having to weed out the male plants in a crop. To feminize seeds, female clones are selected. Under standard conditions these clones do not produce

specific high required. It can be mind-boggling for the beginner. There are over 250 branded seed strains available, with at least another 300 unbranded. Potentially the list is endless, as growers experiment with cross-breeding.

Above: The beauty of the marijuana leaf is visible even in the earliest saplings.

any male flowers, but various methods can make the clones produce abundant male flowers and pollen. The pollen produced by these hermaphrodite herbs is then used to produce feminized seeds.

In 1999, feminized seed pioneers the Dutch Passion Seed Company experimented with 15 varieties of feminized seeds. They started with 30 seeds per variety, with the aim to determine the percentages of female, male and hermaphroditic plants and to compare the uniformity among plants from feminized seeds with those grown from 'regular' seeds. They discovered that certain environmental factors in the first 2–3 weeks of growth, such as higher nitrogen concentration, higher humidity, lower temperatures and more blue light with fewer 'daylight' hours, gave more female plants, whereas a higher potassium concentration gave more males.

While many seed retailers now stock the higher-priced feminized seeds, they remain highly controversial and have split grass growers down the middle, with the opposing camp claiming that they are not 100 per cent guaranteed, and that the process goes against nature.

Pot That Pot
Once the seeds have been obtained they need to be soaked in warm water overnight. Next, pick out the round, fat brown ones and discard the rest. Take the seeds and pot them individually in some rich, black loam compost. Small yoghurt pots are good for this. Ideally, the soil should be kept moist, not wet, and at a temperature of 18°–27°C (64°–87°F). Sprouts should start to appear between 5 and 14 days later. Once the second set of leaves appear, the seedlings should be either re-potted or planted

**Above: It's best to plant seedlings in
separate pots to allow for plenty of growth.**

outdoors in a sunny position, protected from wind
and prying eyes, in early to late spring, depending
on the climate. The seedlings should be planted
about 30cm (1ft) apart to allow for growth, and
kept moist and fertilized. Outdoors, the plants
generally mature in about 4–5 months and are
harvested between September and November.

If the plants are kept indoors, they need to be
in a big enough pot to allow for growth and be
kept in a sunny place. Many of the most potent
strains of cannabis are grown indoors in artificial
conditions. With a set of lights creating artificial
sunshine attached to a timer, it's possible to

> "Marihuana influences Negroes to look at white people in the eye, step on white men's shadows and look at a white woman twice."

Hearst newspapers nationwide, 1934

"I enjoy smoking cannabis and see no harm in it."

Jennifer Aniston

Above: Simple indoor grow areas are relatively easy to set up. Here, the grower has used a mirror to maximise his light source.

create more frequent and stronger crops in a simple cupboard. However, the serious herbalist will want to set up a grow room.

The Green Room

A corner in the basement or attic, or a spare bedroom is the perfect place to start an indoor garden. A 1,000W high intensity discharge (HID) lamp should efficiently illuminate a 2m (6ft) square room with a 1.5m (5ft) ceiling. The plants should be set up about 30cm (1ft) off the ground in containers, and the lamp needs about 30cm (1ft) of space to hang from the ceiling, leaving 1m (3ft) of space for plants to grow. If stuck with a low ceiling, cloning, bending, pruning and using 400W lamps can compensate for the lack of height.

The room should be enclosed, and everything unrelated to the garden should be removed, as furniture and curtains can harbour fungi and moulds. Ideally the floor should be concrete or a smooth surface that can be swept and washed down. The walls, ceiling and floor should be painted with a highly reflective whitewash. Good reflective light will give plants more light energy and will increase an HID lamp's effectiveness by 10–20 per cent.

A constant air circulation and supply of fresh air are also essential. A vent can be simply an open door, window or a duct vented to the outside. An oscillating free-stand fan works well for circulation, but it shouldn't be set in a fixed position, as it could cause windburn or dry out young seedlings and clones. Plumbing is an essential aspect of any grow room, particularly if hydroponics are involved. A 3 x 3m (10 x 10ft) garden could use more than 225l (50gal) a week, and carrying water is hard work. It's much easier to run in a hose with an on/off valve.

There are some tools an indoor gardener must have, one of which is a hygrometer, which measures humidity. If the humidity is too high and causing sickly growth, a hygrometer will warn the unwary horticulturist.

Finally, the seedlings and rooted clones can be moved into the room. Huddle them closely together under the lamp, making sure the HID is not too close that it burns their leaves. 400W lamps should be 46cm (18in) above seedlings and clones, 600W lamps 60cm (2ft) away, and 1000W lamps 76cm (2ft 6in) away.

One Dutch technique for creating vast crops in a very small space is the 'sea of green'. This system involves small plants forced to mature early and produce the fastest crop of buds and flowers. After one crop has grown another is planted beneath it, creating a miniature rainforest canopy with the top plants maturing faster, then being harvested to allow the plants underneath to grow, so a continuous crop is created. It's not the size of the plant that is important in growing, but rather the maturity and quality that counts. The flowering of indoor plants can take anywhere from 6–9 weeks, depending on the strain, and growing the plants under a simple 400W light has the capability of producing more than a half a pound of grass every two months. However, to get the biggest, best and most mind-blowing harvest, the complex worlds of enforced growing and hydroponics need to be employed.

Hydroponic Heaven

Hydroponics (literally 'water works') is a system of agriculture in which plants are grown using water rather than soil. The process dates as far back as the ancient Babylonians and Aztecs, who grew crops on giant floating rafts on lakes. In

1699, John Woodward, a fellow of the Royal Society, developed the first man-made hydroponic nutrient solution. Over the centuries various scientists developed horticulture not using soil, but inert mediums, such as gravel, sand, peat or sawdust, which had a nutrient solution added containing all the essential elements needed by the plant for its normal growth and development.

Hydroponics is still a relatively young science, and has only been used on a commercial basis for about 40 years. Despite this, it helps feed millions of people, and units can be found flourishing in the deserts of Israel, Lebanon and Kuwait, on the islands of Ceylon and the Philippines, and on the rooftops of Calcutta. NASA has even investigated hydroponics as a means of growing food in space for long-term projects such as the first men on Mars, a trip that would require at least three years.

For the modern grass grower, hydroponics allows complete control over an indoor crop. Liquid nutrients and oxygen are pumped into inert rockwool, normally used for roof insulation, creating a reservoir underneath the growing platform.

Added to this are lights. To grow small plants, fluorescent lights are good, but to grow any large or high-light plants, the brightness of HID lamps is essential. HIDs out-perform fluorescents in efficiency, spectral balance and brilliance. High-pressure sodium lamps are usually bought ready to install and are cheap to run, with a

400W unit on for 12 hours a day costing around £2 ($3.5) per week. The timed artificial sunlight and temperature create the perfect conditions for growth. This results in more all-year-round harvests, as growers are no longer reliant on external weather conditions, and much stronger highs as the plant's maturity can be forced. Of course, for the beginner this is a major investment, both in space, time and money, but the serious grower will reap just rewards with a little dedication.

Above: Cannabis is extremely hardy and can grow wild practically anywhere. Right: And where there's weed there's those willing to gather and smoke it!

Harvesting the Herb

Once the male plants have been identified they can be discarded, with a few left for breeding purposes. Approximately four months after planting, the majority of the female plants are pulled, with a few left to flower and seed.

Personal Highs:
Sensimilla Family

The weed can be a wonderful thing. This moving letter is from a woman who wrote to the Canadian Commission of Enquiry into the Non-Medical Use of Drugs, and was printed in their 1970 interim report.

'In his bid to solve the generation gap, our middle son brought a packet of marihuana to us for a Christmas present a year ago. I was slightly horrified because I hoped, like most other parents, that my children were not using it. I was not prepared to try it then. However, with [considerable] persuasion... I tried it, as did his father, brother and sister.

'Not too much happened the first time, except that a kind of mellowness settled over the family. We smiled a lot and listened to music that seemed somehow less forbidding than when the kids played the records previously. The next night we smoked the rest of it and the place started swinging. It was really marvellous. Everyone managed to talk together, about trivialities mainly; there was no tendency to put down anyone. Opportunities to complain or dig at the lack of academic diligence that was always part of the previous conversations with this boy were ignored, and father in particular listened to some of his ideas with a semblance of civility. That alone made the experience worthwhile. The family that night was closer together than any time I can recall. I was greatly surprised to see that what had seemed to be many hours was only an hour and a half. We were all very happy together, and went off to our rooms feeling as if we loved each other for the human beings we were, not for mere points on a scale of achievement.

'For the first time in years my husband and I talked for an hour or more about work, plans, memories, problems and possible solutions – all things we never discussed with each other because of the old scientist/humanist conflict and the rivalries that develop between people in conflicting fields of interest. The miracle is that he seemed also to be a human being, and not only a work machine that ignored people, and particularly his family. I must have seemed somewhat more reasonable to him too, as he did not try to depreciate my interests.

'The real miracle followed when we had intercourse. Instead of the dull, perfunctory act it had become, usually indulged in on my part because it made it possible to get out of it the next night, sex was something splendid. All the old routine thrust and counterthrust to get it over with as soon as possible disappeared. The sensation was extraordinary, each second was a kind of new adventure, each movement an experience, and the climaxes beautiful beyond description. It was far more beautiful than the first weeks of marriage, and the glow of

fulfilment lasted throughout the next day. It was both a physical and intellectual rediscovery between two people who knew each other too well for too long.'

Truly, the family that smokes together stays together.

> **"The next night we smoked the rest of it and the place started swinging. It was marvellous."**

Above: This professional Dutch set-up for drying cannabis has trays below to collect any falling pollen or buds.

Sensimilla flower buds mature around 6–12 weeks after flowering starts. The best time to harvest sensimilla is when THC production has peaked but not started degrading.

Indica and indica/sativa hybrids tend to go through 5–10 weeks of rapid bud formation before levelling off. Harvesting should take place 1–3 weeks after growth slows. Sativa varieties – such as Thai, Mexican, Colombian and African – tend to form buds at an even rate throughout flowering, with no obvious decline in growth rate. Buds at the top of the plant can reach peak potency a few days or weeks before buds on lower branches, and require several harvests, whereas long-season plants, such as Thai Haze, can flower for several months.

The pulled plants should then be tied up and hung upside down in a dark, warm place to dry them out. For best results, drying should be slow with circulating, temperate, dry air. When dried slowly, over 2–3 weeks, moisture evaporates evenly into the air, yielding uniformly dry buds with minimal THC decomposition. Generally, these buds have a smooth, sweet-tasting smoke. Tops dried too slowly in humid air (above 80 per cent) tend to contract fungus and burn poorly. Some paper placed underneath will catch any falling seeds or flowers.

While the drying takes place, the remaining female plants still growing should be checked for flowering. When this occurs, the pollination process can be aided by shaking the male plants over them to aid fertilization, but this is not always necessary. The males can then be thrown away and the female plants pulled up when they start to wilt. These are also hung up to dry (impatient growers can microwave them), and the fertilized seeds should be collected and used to plant the next crop.

Once the drying process is completed, the seeds, flowers, leaves and stalks should be separated. The stalks can be used to make a soothing herbal tea while the flowers and leaves are saved for smoking or cooking. Then sit back and enjoy.

And finally, although cannabis is hardy and self-regulating, 'It's wise to check plants every couple of days,' advised one grower. 'And it's nice to talk to them and pass along good karma.' Remember, herbal horticulture isn't just a hobby, it's a way of life.

Above: At the end of a busy day harvesting comes the final reward for your labour and time to relax after all the hard work! A couple of freaky farmers light up to enjoy the benefits of their crop via a large chillum.

Chapter 2

Maui Wowie Music

Renowned for its creative influence, cannabis has inspired musicians throughout history. Regardless of styles, whether jazz, reggae, rock, pop or hip-hop, marijuana makes beautiful music.

Maui Wowie Music

Even as far back as the 1890s, Pancho Villa's pot-smoking Mexican revolutionaries were singing about sensimilla in traditional songs like 'La Cucaracha' ('The Cockroach'). The lyrics tell how *'La cucaracha ya no puede caminar, porque no tiene marihuana por fumar'*, or 'The cockroach can't walk any more, because he doesn't have any marijuana to smoke.' But the first musical movement to really rave about reefer was the jazz of the Twenties and Thirties.

The Golden Age of Jazz

Jazz had its own phraseology for dope with everything from muggles to vipers (stoners) and Mezz (named after clarinettist and super-dealer Milton Mezzrow). Classic musicians like Louis Armstrong recorded the instrumental 'Muggles' in 1928 with pianist Earl 'Fatha' Hines in Chicago. Satchmo's best-known reefer tune was a warm, lilting blues instrumental that passes the melody round like a joint. In 1932 Cab Calloway praised the pot dealer in 'Reefer Man'. Two years later, Stuff Smith and his Onyx Club Boys sang,

Above: Louis Armstrong, like many jazz players, used to smoke large amounts of what he called 'Mary Warner'.

'Dreamed about a reefer/Five feet long/The mighty Mezz, but not too strong/You'll be high, but not for long/If you'se a viper...' in the classic 'You'se a Viper'. Piano supremo Fats Waller recorded a cover version he called 'The Reefer Song' in 1943.

Vipers were also the subject of Sidney Bechet's 1938 hit, 'Viper Mad'. The New Orleans legend roped in Noble Sissle's Swingsters' to sing, 'Wrap your chops 'round this stick of tea/Blow this gage and get high with me/Good tea is my weakness, I know it's bad/It sends me, gate, and I can't wait, I'm viper mad.' It was featured on the soundtrack to Woody Allen's 1999 jazz comedy, *Sweet and Lowdown*.

The same year, Jazz Gillum and his Jazz Boys recorded 'Reefer Head Woman', featuring Big Bill Broonzy on guitar and Washboard Sam on, er, washboard: 'I got a Reefer Headed Woman/She fell right down from the sky (good Lord)/I got a Reefer Headed Woman/She fell right down from the sky/Lord, I gots to drink me two fifths of whisky/Just to get half as high.' Four decades later, perennial rockers Aerosmith recorded a version on their 1979 album *Night In The Ruts*, proving that great tunes never die.

Top Rankin' Roots

With reefer's strong links with Rastafarianism, it seemed almost compulsory for reggae stars to sing about the sacred herb. The biggest name, Bob Marley, managed to raise the three Rs – reggae, Rastafarianism and reefer – from a small

Jamaican cult to a global phenomena. His timeless masterpieces all supported and promoted the use of ganja, from 'Easy Skanking' – 'Excuse me while I light my spliff' – and 'African Herbsman' (1970) to 1973's 'I Shot the Sheriff' (*see* Top 50 World's Greatest Potheads). Bob Marley and his backing band, the Wailers, became a stadium-filling act and toured the world tokin' and teaching, singing and preaching.

Marley's fellow Wailer, Peter Tosh, created the rallying cry for the pro-pot movement, 'Legalize It', on his first solo album for Columbia Records in 1976: 'Legalize it, don't criticize it/ Legalize it, and I'll advertise it.' Tosh, who was gunned down in Jamaica in 1987, explained, 'Only de small man go to bloodclaat jail for 'erb. Man must get 'erb cause man keep de earth runnin' till today.' The track has been covered by endless bands since, notably by Birmingham-based reggae superstars UB40 in 1998.

Bob Marley died from cancer in Miami on 11 May 1981, aged 36. At his funeral, his widow, and Wailers backing singer, Rita, symbolically placed a stalk of sensimilla in the coffin.

The Bob Marley-written 'One Draw' track on Rita's album, *Who Feels It Knows It* (1980, re-released in 1992), indicated an end to Rita's mourning. This infectious pro-ganja tune was banned in Jamaica on release, but made musical history as the first reggae single to top the US Disco charts. The chorus inspired and was sampled by reefer rappers Cypress Hill for 'I Wanna Get High'.

Left: Roots singer, Peter Tosh, on stage in symbolic handcuffs enjoying de 'erb. Above: 'Dreadlock soldier' Bob Marley spreads the Rastafarian gospel.

Above: A Rastafarian enjoys a puff at the Notting Hill Carnival in London. Reggae and reefer are forever entwined.

Bob and Rita's son Ziggy continued his parents' tradition with his, and the Melody Makers', 'Herbs an' Spices' from their 1991 *Jahmekya* album: 'Herbs an' herb an' herb an' spices an' herbs/Give it to me, give it to me, give it to me, give it to me/Spices an' herb, whoa, revolution/Yes, man a revolution…' Four years later Marley Junior recorded 'In the Flow' on the day after the Bob Marley 50th birthday celebrations: 'Politicians fighting to stop I from lighting/But in harmony, we'll smoke the tree.' Ziggy even went on to cover his dad's classic 'African Herbsman' on his 1993 album *Joy and Blues*.

The list of reggae performers singing about the sacred 'erb is practically endless: Jacob Miller's 'Tired Fe Lick Weed In a Bush', Bountykiller's 'Smoke The Herb', Baja Jedd's 'Ganja Smokin', 'Light My Spliff' by Red Dragon, 'Sensimilla Prosecution' by Buju Banton, and U Roy's classic 'Chalice In The Palace'.

In 1980 Duckie Simpson, Mykal Rose and Sandra 'Puma' Jones, AKA Black Uhuru, recorded the *Sinsemilla* album. The trio were the first reggae group to win a Grammy and were a powerful live draw in their day, backed by Sly 'n' Robbie, who produced the classic album and title track: 'I've got a stalk of sinsemilla growing in my back yard...' Their second album continued the ganja theme with the track 'Puff She Puff'.

In the following year, 1981, The Mighty Diamonds politely asked if we'd 'Pass the Kouchie' and scored a Jamaican hit with it. A kouchie, kutchie or couchie is a ceremonious pipe or chalice used for smoking sensi. In the UK, one-hit wonders Musical Youth famously covered the song in 1982, but – fearing outrage that young children would be singing the praises of marijuana – changed the title to 'Dutchie', which makes no sense at all, since a Dutch oven cannot easily be passed from the left-hand side.

Other kutchie tracks include legendary producer Lee 'Scratch' Perry's 'Kutchie Skank', Dillinger's 'Bring The Cutchie Come' and 'Couchie' by Triston Palma.

Paul Love, AKA Jah Screw, had been the selector for U-Roy's sound system before going on to team up with DJ Ranking Joe to produce records. They then proceeded to recruit Barrington 'Broader-than-Broadway' Levy to sing on their first single, 1985's 'Under Mi Sensi', a wild tune which launched a blistering attack on governmental hypocrisy over the weed biz: 'Babylon, you na like ganja man/But we bring the foreign currency 'pon the island.' It remains an enduring anthem, with Beenie Man's 'Jungle Dub X Project Remix' version becoming a UK club hit in 1994.

Patrick George Anthony Barrett, better known by the name Tony Rebel – one of Jamaica's top modern DJs – delivered one of the most erudite and cutting pro-ganja raps of recent years with his 1991 hit 'The Herb': 'Good sensimilla, it used to run this land/But since the other day, them a deal with substitution/Now the crop called cocaine bring pure destruction/That's why this morning, me get up and me write three letter/Come, me a seh, one addressed to the Prime Minister/Me say, the next one addressed to the Security Minister/Me never done the one to the Commissioner/ Because them, them're hypocrites and counfounder/'Cause how the hell them a going to fight against sensimilla?/And it put a poor people plot 'pon fire/Now, we used to plant it enough in Jamaica/And they burn it down with 'nuff police and soldier/And them import the coke fe mash up we future/But, you see the Herb/ It just me brain it preserve/ You see, the Herb/It make I-man observe/You see, the Herb/It just a-strengthen me nerve...'

Above: The deceased rapper Biggie Smalls AKA The Notorious B.I.G.

1994 saw stadium skankers UB40's Ali and Robin Campbell team up with Pato Banton for a ragga version of the old Equals hit 'Baby Come Back'. It reached Number One in the UK, thanks to Banton's lyrical toasting about his 'bag of sensi'.

Rapper's Delight

While most of the grass-inspired jazz and reggae tunes were mostly about love, laughter and lightin' up, the Eighties saw the rise of a new, harsher, deadlier musical weed wave, gangsta rap.

New bands like Public Enemy came on harder than their late Seventies rap predecessors, the Sugar Hill Gang and Grandmaster Flash. The majority of the new gangsta rap came out of East LA and New York with two 9-millis blazing and singing about bitches, blow and bling. An intense, and deadly, rivalry developed between the East and West Coast scenes, which resulted in numerous rappers and producers killed, most notoriously Tupac Shakur and Biggie Smalls AKA The Notorious B.I.G.

The highly political New York-based Public Enemy consisted of Chuck D, DJ Terminator X (Norman Lee Rogers), Professor Griff (Richard Griff) and Flavor Flav (William Drayton). The group formed in 1982 and has been met with controversy ever since. The band endorsed Black Muslim leader Louis Farrakhan, and anti-Semitic remarks made by Griff forced him out of the band. Flavor Flav's constant run-ins with the law reached a high/low point in 1996 while he was riding his bike in the Bronx. Police officers noticed a large bulge in his jacket and stopped him. They found a kilo brick of marijuana. A little tricky to explain it was purely for personal use. Then again…

Into this scene came Andre Young, a young rhymer who started rapping in the early Eighties at house parties with the World Class Wreckin' Crew. He wore a doctor's mask on stage, and thus Dr Dre, rap's greatest record producer, was born. In 1986 he met Ice Cube, and together they teamed up with former drug dealer Eazy-E to form Niggaz With Attitude (NWA). Inspired by the success of Public Enemy, NWA were extremely influential themselves, celebrating the amoral excesses of

Above: Public Enemy's Flavor Flav's dress sense hasn't improved with age.

gang life, and their 1989 debut album *Straight Outta Compton* (an impoverished LA neighbourhood) exploded into massive sales. While many rappers loved smoking chronic, Ice Cube rapped a different tune on the track 'Express Yourself':

The *Kama Sutra* of Cannabis

Can sensimilla send smokers into higher states of sexual ecstasy, or is it simply a case of not tonight, Mary Jane? One infamous book, the *Kama Sutra*, addressed man's eternal struggle: sex or sleep?

The *Kama Sutra* – literally 'rules of love' – is the world's oldest existing textbook of erotic lore. Although downright obscene in places, its fans claim that it is not a piece of ancient porn, rather an impartial and systematic study of one of the essential aspects of existence.

This ancient Joy of Sex guide listed a whole host of exotic, not to mention eclectic, aphrodisiacs. Fancy creating a massage ointment of powdered herbs gathered in a human skull, or anointing your penis with milk hedge, red arsenic and sulphur? If you're hungry for love (or you've simply got the munchies), there's rams testicles baked in sugared milk. But if all this is too much, just remember, 'By holding in one's left hand a peacock's or hyena's eye, wrapped in gold, one

finds success in love.' Luckily posterity did not take on all the *Kama Sutra*'s love drugs, but one has made it to the present day: bhang.

Bhang is the *Kama Sutra*'s answer to the bedtime spliff – a potent cocktail of cannabis leaves and buds steeped in water and pulverized with milk and spices. Bhang has survived the ages to be one of the most popular enhancers of the luv experience. As author/playwright Norman Mailer said, 'Sex without pot is never quite as good as sex with pot', and it seems that many would agree. 74 per cent of men and 62 per cent of women interviewed in Erich Goode's *The Marijuana Smokers* said they enjoyed sex more when they were high. Stories of marathon sex sessions abound. As one sexy stoner reports, 'We

Above: In the mood for love, or just a big bag of tortilla chips?

came together on a huge round bed and writhed around in ecstasy for an immeasurable amount of time…we must have covered the entire Kama Sutra…the effect was sheer bliss!', or to put it more succinctly, 'Do not use Viagra, use cannabis instead,' advises the UK lobby group, the Sexual

It seems that spliffs are decidedly sexy. One 27 year-old divorcee is only able to orgasm once she has had a toke, and 'Zed' too has specific uses for her weed: 'I really only use drugs for enjoying sex more… the combination of my partner's renewed enthusiasm, tossing aside any inhibitions, eagerness for exploration and unstoppable drive, with my own heightened sensitivity and wild abandon leads to more

Below: The flesh may be willing but the spirit is weak. Too much marijuana may mean getting a good night's sleep rather than getting it on.

However, most scientists agree that in physiological terms marijuana is not an aphrodisiac; rather, it dulls the sexual areas and decreases desire. Constantinos Miras, a Greek pharmacologist, studied how cannabis decreased the sexual activity of rats, and botanist Norman Taylor heartily agrees: 'As to being a sex-excitant, marijuana appears to be just the opposite.' Dr McCoid, who runs a Glasgow men's sexual health clinic, concurs: 'Initially, cannabis acts as a stimulant, but heavy use lowers the production of the male hormone testosterone, and that leads to a lowering of sex drive', and even impotence in users as young as 17. Not so much brewer's droop as stoner's flop.

Biology aside, what of the story of the young experimenter who was in the midst of being seduced by her bong-loving boyfriend when she saw little green men coming through the window to attack her? Perhaps they were Bhangi, the guardian spirits of the sacred hemp plant, within which, so Hindu tradition holds, resides the brooding spirit of the great yogi and ascetic Mahadev.

By definition an aphrodisiac is a substance that increases sexual desire. Cannabis does not appear to increase desire so much as enhance the toker's experience of sex: 'It helps me focus on what's going on, so it becomes the centre of my existence.' Cannabis activates what is latent in the sexy stoner – in some cases this is 'loose, free and wild, and abandoned, and reckless and freaky', while in other cases it's little green men at the window poised to attack. It all depends where you are cuming from.

Others report energy interchanges with their partner and whole-body sensations. One 31-year-old male research scientist reported how 'I can feel myself actually fusing with the other person – it is difficult to know even anatomically what part of myself is me and what part is the woman.' Such experiences echo the ongoing full-body orgasmic experience of Tantric sexuo-spiritual ecstasy – 'He forgets who he is, and she forgets who she is,' wrote Robert E. Svoboda in his 1986 book, *Aghora: At The Left Hand Of God*. Bhang devotees achieve a similar state through drinking or smoking their sacred weed: 'By sipping, the bhang reaches and soothes the Shiva-Shakti or Shiva-spirit in the sipper,' according to J.M. Campbell's *On the Religion of Hemp* (1893). Perhaps the cocktail of bhang and sex really does offer a motorway to enlightenment.

And so, although cannabis has no scientifically proven aphrodisiac qualities, in most cases a spliff before bed is a recipe for sex. It's not about chemistry within the body so much as chemistry between partners, sparked up and intensified by marijuana's magical ability to '…provoke a more sensual (or aesthetic) kind of concentration, a detailed articulation of minute areas, an ability to adopt play postures,' enthused Alexander Trocchi, novelist and self-confessed drug addict. 'What can be more relevant in the act of love?'

However, as expert smoker Erich Goode warns, even the most serious devotee of bhang must be moderate if he wants to explore all the *Kama Sutra*'s 64 lessons of love: 'After two or three "good" joints, the only erotic experience the pothead will have will be in his dreams.'

45

attitude got them an official warning from the FBI, and in 1989 Ice Cube quit after financial disagreements. Dre quit the band the following year, after his new business partner at Death Row records, Suge Knight, put a gun to the head of NWA's manager and ordered him to free Dre from his contract. Eazy-E went on to run Ruthless

Left: Bad boy rapper and actor Ice Cube. Below: The most respected rap producer on the planet, Dr Dre.

"I still express, yo, I don't smoke weed or sens/Cause it's known to give a brother brain damage/And brain damage on the mic don't manage…' Dr Dre produced the single, but obviously didn't share these sentiments, as he was to demonstrate on his solo album *The Chronic*. The band's success was assured, but NWA had problems. Their 'Fuck tha police'

Records and managed many bands including Bone Thugs-N-Harmony, but died of AIDS in March 1995, aged just 31.

The Doctor will see you now

In 1992 Dr Dre's first solo album, *The Chronic*, featured a big green leaf on the sleeve. Chronic started out as slang for weed laced with coke, but it soon became synonymous with incredibly potent marijuana. Dre's album had numerous skits between the songs, including 'The $20 Sack Pyramid', a game show where the prize is a bag of pot. This hip-hop landmark covered the similar violent territory recorded by NWA, but Dre found some exciting new voices to verbalize it, including Snoop Doggy Dogg (see Top 50 Greatest Potheads). Snoop Dogg is no stranger to the weed himself, having been busted at least twice for possession, once at a Los Angeles comedy club in 1998, and while on tour in 2001. He was even named *High Times'* Stoner of the Year in 2002. *The Chronic's* real revelation, however, was in the grooves. Dre blended jazz, funk and soul elements into its hip-hop goulash, sampling Donny Hathaway, Isaac Hayes and George Clinton's ex-band Parliament. The final track, 'The Roach', tells it like it is to the tune of 'P-Funk': 'Make my butt the chronic/I wants to get fucked up.'

The Chronic was almost a social worker album. When asked whether he thought herb had helped mellow out a lot of the thug mentality in hip-hop, Snoop Dogg replied, 'On

Above: Snoop Dogg is king bling Huggy Bear in the 2004 *Starsky and Hutch* movie.

the real. When me and Dre put chronic on the map, we took crack out of the black community. It's erasing the crack that was killing a lot of our people and sending homies to the jailhouse. Now it's more controlled, civilized and more about money and bitches and just smoking. That's the cool shit. Before that, the crackhead niggas was just running wild out there.'

However, Dr Dre wasn't always on the ball with his social conscience. His production of RBX's 1996 'Blunt Time' from *The Aftermath* album recommends: 'Blunt time – pull out your Philly/Sip a glass of 'gnac, reload your nine-milli/Dancin', puffin', sippin' or set trippin'/Dimes keep on flippin', flippin'…' Combining hash, alcohol and semi-automatic pistols has 'recipe for disaster' stamped all over it. Dre continued to rap about reefer in 1995, with 'Keep Their Heads Ringin'' paying homage to an iconic stoner duo: 'But I smoke 'em like grass, just like Cheech and Chong.'

'I Don't Give a Fuck'

When Dre heard a young Detroit rapper freestyling on a Los Angeles radio station in 1997, he put out a manhunt for the Michigan rhymer. Shortly thereafter, Dre signed up the white, blond badass Marshall Mathers, AKA Eminem. 'It was an honour to hear the words out of Dre's mouth that he liked my shit,' Eminem said. 'Growing up, I was one of the biggest fans of NWA, from putting on the sunglasses and looking in the mirror and lip-syncing to wanting to be Dr Dre, to be Ice Cube. [Dre] is the biggest hip-hop producer ever.' While Eminem raps about many things, weed has not been the highest priority. However, on his *Slim Shady* album he sings, 'Mental problems got me snorting coke and smoking weed again.' And Eminem's ex-wife, Kimberley Mathers, has been busted on numerous occasions for possession of marijuana and cocaine. 'I believe that a lot of people can relate to my shit – whether white, black, it doesn't matter,' explained the troubled rapster. 'Everybody has been through some shit, whether it's drastic or not so drastic. Everybody gets to the point of "I Don't Give a Fuck",' a track from the *Slim Shady* album.

Previously, in 1996, Eminem had released his debut album, *Infinite*. 'I felt like *Infinite* was like a demo that just got pressed up.' After being crushed by the universal panning *Infinite* got, Eminem began working on his homegrown *Slim Shady* album. 'I had nothing to lose, but something to gain,' Eminem said. 'I lashed out on everybody who talked shit about me.' He then won second place in The Rap Coalition's LA freestyle competition. During the trip, Eminem made his major radio debut on the *Wake Up Show with Sway and Tech*. Realizing it was make or break, Eminem delivered a furious medley of lyrics that blew away his hosts and radio audience. 'I felt like it's my time to shine,'

Right: Marshall Mathers AKA Slim Shady AKA Eminem. Homophobic or hydroponic?

"Looking at fires when high, by the way, especially through one of those prism kaleidoscopes which image their surroundings, is an extraordinarily moving and beautiful experience."

Carl Sagan

"There's been no top authority saying what marijuana does to you. I really don't know that much about it. I tried it once, but it didn't do anything to me."

John Wayne

he recalled, 'I have to rip this. At that time, I felt that it was a life or death situation.' It worked, and Dre tracked him down. Eminem has gone on to be one of the biggest and most controversial names in rap. Accusations of misogyny and homophobia haven't stopped him crossing over to the mainstream, and he looks set to be around for a long time.

All of Dre's collaborators came together for the legendary 2000 *Up in Smoke Tour* (named after the classic Cheech and Chong stoner movie). It was the rap tour to end all rap tours: Snoop Dogg, Eminem, Ice Cube and Dr Dre all on stage together in a spectacular show that praised blunts, buds and beer in their unique styles. The show was put onto DVD in 2001, and is considered one of the best rap gigs ever.

The only truly credible white rap act before Eminem was not Vanilla Ice, but rather the Beastie Boys. The beer-swilling brats raised hell in the Countdown studios while recording their explosive 1986 debut album *License to Ill* with cans of beer and fat joints in their hands. During their 1987 concert at the Jaap Edenhal, Holland, the Beasties were stoned *als een garnaal,* 'like a shrimp' as the Dutch say, while declaring that they had a wonderful afternoon in that Mecca of marijuana, the Bulldog café in Amsterdam. Mike D, Ad-Rock and MCA looked to cheeba for their massively influential second album, 1989's *Paul's Boutique*. While heavily under the influence of producers the Dust Bros and the sweet smoke of sensi, the trio lyrically littered the album with weed references, including 'Car Thief': 'Space cake cookies, I discover who I am/I'm a dusted old bummy Hurdy Gurdy Man' and '3 Minute Rule': 'I smoke cheeba, it helps me with my brain/I might be a little dusted, but I'm not insane.'

Time to get Blunted

A band who were 'Insane in the Brain' were Cypress Hill. They kicked in the rap scene's door with their self-titled 1991 album. Right from the start, The Hill was all about the buds. Their debut tracks included 'Something for the Blunted', 'Light Another' and 'Stoned Is the Way of the Walk': 'I'm the freaka, the one who freaks the funk/Sen got the Philly an' he's gonna light the blunt...'

The band was formed in Southeast LA by American-Italian DJ Muggs (Larry Muggerud), Mexican-Cuban South Gate, Californian native B-Real (Louis Freeze) and Cuban Sen Dog (Senen Reyes). They took their name from Cypress Avenue, a street that ran through their neighbourhood.

Cypress Hill's 1993 album, *Black Sunday*, is not only a masterpiece and one of the biggest-selling rap albums of all time, but it's also one big ode to the green grass of life. It includes the hit single, 'Insane in the Brain', 'Hits From the Bong' and 'I Wanna Get High', based on Bob Marley's 'One Draw': 'Yes I smoke shit, straight off the roach clip/I roach it, roll the blunt at once to approach it/Forward motion make you sway like

Above: Cypress Hill's *Black Sunday* album mourns a bad day when they ran out of grass.

the ocean/The herb is more than just a powerful potion/What's the commotion, yo I'm not joking around/People learning about what they're smoking/My oven is on high, when I roast the quail/Tell Bill Clinton to go and inhale.' The live version ends with the chant, 'If ya wanna legalize the herb, let me hear you say pom, pom, pom.'

The Hill appeared on the second Lollapalooza 'indie band' tour in 1992 and played with bands like Pearl Jam, exposing them to a whole new alternative rock audience. The following year

Cypress Hill teamed up again with Pearl Jam on the *Judgement Night* soundtrack (starring pro-chronic comedian Denis Leary). The album also saw them joining forces with alternative rock gods Sonic Youth to record 'I Love You Mary Jane': 'When I shift, I kick to go/Like a fat drunk and I light up a fat spliff/Take a whiff/Can you smell that in the air?/When the smoke come out the building from everywhere.'

Unsurprisingly, the band became spokesmen for the legalization of hemp, hooking up in 1991 with the National Organization to Reform Marijuana Laws (NORML) and, in the words of *High Times* magazine, 'igniting a revolution'.

Riding the Can-I-Bus

The Jamaican-born rapper Germaine Williams took his love of green to the extreme, and not only sang about cheeba but even changed his stage name to Cannibus. His 1998 debut album *Can-I-Bus* was produced by ex-Fugee Wyclef Jean and delivered 'twin turbine rhymes with four thousand pounds of thrust' that are unambiguously powered by the herb. The track 'Buckingham Palace' is undoubtedly inspired by U-Roy's classic reggae chant, 'Chalice In The Palace': 'I stand outside the gates of Buckingham Palace/Selling reefer, puffin the chalice with the Beefeaters/ Getting so high that whenever I drop shit/It'll land on the window of your airplane cockpit…' His inspired chorus with the crowd goes, 'When I say "Can-I" you say "Bus"/Can-I (BUS!) Can-I (BUS!)…' Cannibus also became

notorious for an intense rivalry with pop hip-hop balladeer LL Cool J, while releasing four further albums, *2000 BC, C: True Hollywood Stories, Mic Club: The Curriculum* and *Rip The Jacker*.

Bizarrely, Cannibus took his own advice from his song 'Draft Me', threw away his musical career and joined the United States Army in 2003. However, winning Arabic hearts and minds may prove tricky if the rapper sings his own lyrics to them: "I wanna fight for my country/Jump in a Humvee and murder those monkeys… Lurkin' to leave y'all with bloody red turbans/Screamin' "Jihad!" while y'all pray to a false god…'

Mean Green

Meanwhile, other, mellower rappers were still on the beam about blunts. In 1991 Cool Hand Loc's second album, *Delicious Vinyl*, had the track 'Mean Green': 'When a believer gets the fever for the flavour of the cheeba/Don't you sweat it, I can get it, I got my home boy's beeper number/If you wanna get some of the chronic, supersonic/Yo, my man's got that high-powered hydroponic… Don't mention cocaine, heroin or speed/In the same breath as weed, because nobody ever OD'ed/Puffing reefer, *cannabis sativa*, hemp or the cheeba, and I'm a believer.' A perfect case for legalization if ever there was one.

The Disposable Heroes of Hiphoprisy updated the Dead Kennedys' punk classic 'California Über Alles' in 1992, on their 'Hypocrisy Is The

Greatest Luxury'. They added the lyrics: 'Knock knock at your front door, hey guess who?/It's the suede denim secret police/They've come to your house for your long-haired niece/Gonna take her off to a camp/'Cause she's been accused of growing hemp.'

Method Man – a member of New York rap group the Wu-Tang Clan – recorded the seemingly obscurely titled 'Tical' single in 1994. 'In every part of New York there is someone who makes up different slang words that just happen to catch on,' explained Clifford Smith, AKA Method Man. 'In Staten Island we used to call weed "method". Then my man Lounger cut it down to "metical". And then, over the course of time it got cut down to "tical".' The lyrics set the tone with the chorus: 'What's that shit that they be smokin'?/Tical, tical, tical/Pass it over here... tical, tical, tical/What's that shit the niggaz smokin? Tical... tical, tical/Pass it over here... tical, tical, tical.' Method Man followed it up with his *Tical 2000: Judgement Day* album and teamed up with fellow East Coast hip-hopper Red Man to rap 'How High'.

Red Man, AKA Reggie Noble, out of Newark, New Jersey, explained rolling etiquette in 'How To Roll A Blunt' from his *Whut? Thee* album: 'Lick the blunt and then the Philly blunt middle you split/Don't have a razor blade, use ya fuckin' fingertips/Crack the bag and then you pour the whole bag in/Spread the ism around until the ism reach each end/Take your finger and your thumb from tip to tip/Roll it in a motion then the top

piece you lick/Seal it, dry it wit ya lighter if ya gotta/The results, mmmm....proper.' That same year, 1992, saw Gang Starr explain tokin' manners with their informative 'Take Two and Pass': 'I'm in love with Mary Jane she keeps me large/ So don't hog it, let's get it moving real fast/Everybody just chill and take like two pulls and pass...'

Artis Ivey Junior wisely passed on his birth name and changed it to Coolio, and consequently broke through with his 1994 *It Takes A Thief* album. It includes 'Smokin' Stix', about the dubious practice of dunking joints in 'some kind of embalming fluid', which, as the lyrics make clear, is not recommended. Coolio later went on to profess 'I'm In Love With Mary Jane'.

Another lover of old MJ was Master P, the Southern hip-hop soldier. His first independent album in 1994, *The Ghetto's Trying to Kill Me*, contained the track 'I Got That Dank' – dank being another hip-hop term for chronic. Master P's lyrical investigations of cash and drugs include 'Dope, Pussy and Money' from *Mama's Bad Boy* (1993) and 'Weed and Money' from the 1997 *Ghetto D* album, which also includes 'Pass Me Da Green': 'I stack greens like cheese/Smoke weed with g's/Sell cream to fiends/And roll with beams...'

Cleveland-based Bone Thugs-N-Harmony broke into the US charts with the eight-track album *Creepin' On Ah Come Up* in 1994. The raw teenage rappers' massively successful album *E. 1999 Eternal* contained a couple of crucial weed raps, 'Buddah Lovaz' and 'Budsmokers Only': 'Gotta get me some hydro, gotta choke/Let me loc with a little bit of smoke in my throat.'

'I Got 5 On It' was a great big phat 1995 hit single for Dru Down, E-40, Richie Rich, Shock G and Spice 1, AKA Luinz. It came from their debut album, *Operation Stackola*: 'I got 5 on it/Grab your 4 and let's get keyed/I got 5 on it/Messin' with that Indo weed…' The following year West Coast rapper B-Legit celebrated the gangsta life in songs such as 'Gotta Buy Your Dope From Us' 'Rollin' Wit Hustlers' and 'Hemp Museum', about a hydroponic growing facility. It seems as if reefer and rap – just like reggae – are, and always will be, inextricably linked.

Rock 'n' Rollin' Up

While jazz, reggae and rap are renowned for 'dope' tunes, pro-marijuana pop songs are also plentiful. As far back as the Sixties, songs like The Troggs' 'Night Of The Long Grass', 'I Can Hear The Grass Grow' by the Move and the Small Faces' 'Itchicoo Park': 'What did you do there?/I got high!' all reflected the mainstream's move on marijuana.

But not everybody was tokin' 'bout a revolution back then. Despite the dubious title and plenty of references that could easily be misinterpreted, the 1963 hit single 'Puff the Magic Dragon' is *not* a song about pot. Folk stars Peter, Paul and Mary denied any connection with the drug, '['Puff' is about] loss of innocence and

having to face an adult world,' co-writer Leonard Lipton stated. 'Believe me, if he [Peter Yarrow] wanted to write a song about marijuana, he would have written a song about marijuana,' confirmed band member Mary Travers. Still, the myth continued when Presidential candidate John Kerry sang 'Puff' along with Peter Yarrow, and mimed toking on a joint at an Iowa house party i January 2004.

Yet others praised pot more blatantly. Beautiful blues belter Janis Joplin was tragically better known for her fondness for booze than blow, but in 1965 she wrote and sang about 'Mary Jane': 'Now when I go to work, I work all day/Always turns out the same/When I bring home my hard-earned pay/I spend my money all on Mary Jane/Mary Jane, Mary Jane, Lord, my Mary Jane.' This early song was recorded with the Dick Oxtot Oakland Athletics Jazz Band and appeared on the soundtrack to the 1974 bio-pic *Janis*.

Joplin's contemporary Bob Dylan insisted, in 1966, that 'Everybody must get stoned' in 'Rainy Day Women Nos 12 & 35', his Number Two hit single, despite being banned on US radio. The following year Country Joe and The Fish's archetypal hippie ballad, 'Bass Strings', proclaimed: 'Hey partner, won't you pass that reefer round?/My world is spinnin', yeah, just got to slow it down/Oh, yes you know I've sure got to slow it down/Get so high this time that you know

Right: Bob Dylan introduced The Beatles to weed in 1964.

Personal Highs:
Peter Lawford

British actor Peter Lawford was quite partial to a toke or two. In fact, his desire for dope got him into more than one jam in his life.

Born in 1923, Lawford was part of the infamous Rat Pack, the gang of singers and actors that included Dean Martin, Sammy Davis Jr, Joey Bishop and 'chairman of the board', Frank Sinatra. The hell-raisers regularly got drunk together and lorded it over Las Vegas throughout the Fifties and Sixties, and all appeared in the original version of *Ocean's Eleven* in 1960.

The Brit lad was romantically linked with loads of leading ladies, including actresses Lana Turner, Ava Gardner, Lee Remick and Kim Novak. But the movie star went on to marry John F. Kennedy's sister, Patricia, in 1954. When

his brother in-law became President, Lawford was invited to fly aboard Air Force One. The actor's manager then allegedly left three marijuana joints on the plane. However, it's doubtful that JFK would have minded, as the President was a purported pothead as well, apparently smoking to ease the pain of his bad back, as well as for fun. Famed for his sexual conquests, the Prez once supposedly smoked marijuana with a nude playgirl while he joked about being too wasted to push the button in case of a nuclear attack.

But it was Lawford who had the most amusing

exploits, at least for readers. According to Margaret Moser's book, *Movie Stars Do the Dumbest Things*, Lawford flew to Rome on a trip. When he arrived he was toting a substantial stash of cocaine, marijuana and hashish. But while waiting in line to pass through customs, Lawford saw a dog and his paranoia kicked in. Convinced that it was a drug-sniffing police dog, he dumped his stash in a nearby rubbish bin. After passing through customs, Lawford was surprised to see the dog jump into a woman's limousine. He promptly raced back into the airport, ran through customs, and, to the amazement of a group of passengers, began rifling through the bin. Perhaps fortunately, the trash had already been taken out. The actor should have known better, as the supposed police dog was in fact a Chihuahua.

This setback didn't put Lawford off, though; he was pro-pot all the way. In 1979 he even sat on NORML's advisory board alongside Hugh Hefner, Hunter S. Thompson and baby expert Dr Benjamin Spock.

One day in the 1970s, the NYPD received a call that Lawford's son, Christopher, was standing on a second-storey ledge outside his father's Manhattan apartment, strung out on heroin and threatening to kill himself. The police arrived, managed to coax the boy inside and hauled him off, along with an enormous marijuana plant. Lawford watched wistfully as the officers left and cried, 'Oh, no – not the plant!' Spoken like a true stoner.

Ironically, the dope-lovin' actor died of a much more pernicious drug, alcohol, when he contracted cirrhosis and kidney failure in 1984.

"[JFK] smoked marijuana with a nude playgirl while he joked about being too wasted to push the button in case of a nuclear attack."

Above: Musicians drove the legalize cannabis campaigns. When Led Zeppelin's Robert Plant was busted, hippies took to the streets.

I'll never come down.' The band recorded two versions, including a tripped-out psychedelic one on their debut album, *Electric Music for the Mind and Body*.

The Pope Smokes Dope

1968 saw two seminal stoner songs released. The first was 'I Like Marijuana' by David Peel and the Lower East Side. 'First I sang about smoking bananas,' said Peel, bizarrely. 'That was a craze like the hula hoop. Then I started singing about marijuana. That was more permanent.' Peel's pot-related output exploded with 'Legalize Marijuana', 'I've Got Some Grass', 'I Want to Get High' and 'Show Me the Way to Get Stoned'. 'I Like Marijuana' was a highlight of Peel's *Have a Marijuana* album; 27 years later, in 1995, Technohead sampled the classic tune in their ravey summer hit 'I Wanna Be A Hippie'. In 1972 Peel was also responsible for the John Lennon-produced song 'The Pope Smokes Dope', a phrase which has been repeated on endless postcards and T-shirts ever since.

At the same time as Peel's original ganja groove was being cut, rockers Steppenwolf warned of the dangers of self-righteous politicians in 'Don't Step on the Grass, Sam'. Written by John Kay for their *The Second* album, it's the story of a guy watching a TV debate about marijuana: 'Sam is saying casually/"I was elected by the masses"/And with that in mind/He starts to unwind/A vicious attack on the finest of grasses.' The song accuses Sam of 'telling lies so long, some believe they're true' and warns 'Don't be such an ass, Sam.' Steppenwolf then went on to sing the praises of their dealer, but warned of the dangers of 'The Pusher': 'You know the dealer, the dealer is a

Above: *Easy Rider* led a pot revolution through film and music.

man/With the love of grass in his hand/Oh but he pusher is a monster/Good God, he's not a natural man.' The song appeared on the 1969 soundtrack for the stoner movie of the Sixties, *Easy Rider*. Another pot-promoting song from the soundtrack was Fraternity of Man's 'Don't Bogart Me'. The song became better known as 'Don't Bogart That Joint', and was a rousing live favourite at Little Feat gigs throughout the

Seventies: 'Roll another one/Just like the other one/This one's burnt to the end/Come on and be a friend.'

In the Seventies other drugs, particularly cocaine and heroin, pushed weed aside as popular song subjects. Punks spat on everything hippie and pot-related, preferring the more subtle aromas of speed and glue-sniffing. Despite this, a few musicians kept the faith, including prog-rockers Hawkind, with their 'Reefer Madness', and Doctor Hook's 1973 ditty, 'Acapulco Goldie'. And while not many people had heard of Pud, as soon as they named themselves after a joint, the Doobie Brothers exploded onto the music scene in 1971 with dope-inspired tracks like 'Cotton Mouth'.

Sweet Leaf

1971 also saw heavy metallists Black Sabbath enter the dope debate with 'Sweet Leaf'. This paean to pot – written by Tony Iommi, Geezer Butler, Bill Ward and Birmingham's Ozzy 'Prince of Darkness' Osbourne – appeared on the album *Masters of Reality*. Essentially it's a love song to the weed of wonder: 'Straight people don't know what you're about/They put you down and shut you out/You gave me a new belief/ And soon the world will love you, sweet leaf.' The song has become a favourite for grass-smoking metal bands across America, all of them bashing out their own versions.

Perennial rocker Neil Young recorded his agricultural anthem 'Homegrown' with his sometime backing group Crazy Horse on his 1977 album *American Stars 'n' Bars*: 'Homegrown is all right with me/Homegrown is the way it should be/Homegrown is a good thing/ Plant that bell and let it ring' sang the man who influenced a whole generation of modern rock.

More recently, post-punks Green Day named themselves after the San Francisco Bay-area slang for a day with lots of green bud where you just sit around taking bong hits and hanging out. Lead singer Billie Joe wrote the song 'Green Day' about his first pot experience, and the group changed its name from Sweet Children to Green Day in 1990, recording the song on their debut album, *1039/Smoothed Out Slappy Hours*.

Another contemporary pro-soft drugs band are the Atlanta-based Black Crowes who, during their 1992 *High As The Moon* tour, sold official Black Crowes rolling papers. The anti-corporate (but not anti-merchandizing) band's lead singer, Chris Robinson, disapproves of the fact that there are people in prison for the possession of one single gram of marijuana.

Brits' Blow

The British music scene hasn't been afraid to get its fingers green either. Numerous pop and rock acts have sung about spliff. Ex-Happy Mondays' lead singer Shaun Ryder's first Black Grape album may be called *It's Great When You're Straight... Yeah*, but on stage, he's one big ad for (or against) a fat, sweet joint. In 1994 Supergrass (named after a police informant rather than a

strong strain of weed) released their debut album, *I Should Coco*. The British trio's first single, 'Caught By The Fuzz', tells the true story of singer Gaz Coombes getting busted at the age of 15: 'I talked to a man who says "Better to tell/Who sold you the blow?"/Well it was no one I know/"If only you'd tell us, we'd let you go"...'

That same year Birmingham popsters Dodgy promoted their second album, *Homegrown* (a theme popularized earlier by Neil Young), which contained a track called 'Grassman', by distributing hemp seeds and grow manuals to journalists. Dodgy indeed. And even Mancunian stadium Britpoppers Oasis included kingsize rolling papers in their merchandizing à la Black Crowes. Oasis's volatile frontman Liam Gallagher hit the headlines in the UK when he was busted in 1997 for cocaine possession. His brother and fellow band member, Noel, then notoriously compared taking drugs to 'having a cup of tea in the morning' – some Lapsang Souchong and a spliff, the perfect way to start the day. Acid jazz funksters Jamiroquai have been demanding the decriminalization of dope for years, with lead singer Jay Kay bitterly railing against the politics: 'They [the Government] begrudge the people the enjoyment of soft drugs.'

A band that obviously did get the 'enjoyment of soft drugs' were the Super Furry Animals. Their 1996 debut album on Creation records, *Fuzzy Logic*, went one further.

Left: Shaun Ryder, Madchester icon and Second Summer of Love survivor.

"I do smoke, but I don't go through all this trouble just because I want to make my drug of choice legal. It's about personal freedom...Seventy-two million people in this country have smoked pot. Eighteen to twenty million in the last year. These people should not be treated as criminals."

Woody Harrelson

"**The drug is really quite a remarkably safe one for humans, although it is really quite a dangerous one for mice and they should not use it.**"

J.W.D. Henderson, Director of the Bureau of Human Drugs, Health and Welfare, Canada

The cover featured multiple portraits of the celebrated fellow Welshman and hash smuggler, Howard Marks, showing the various disguises he adopted while on the run. The album contains a track called 'Hangin' Out with Howard Marks', and Mr Nice even got behind the mixing desk long enough to get a production credit for a mix of their single, 'The Man Don't Give a Fuck'. But he did give enough of a fuck to stick with music for a while, and went on to form the Howard Marks Project, recording the album *Nice 'n' Idle and Jutterjaw* in 1999. Tracks included 'Mr Nasty', 'Stoned', 'My First E' and 'Je Suis Marijuana'. The techno title track opens with someone taking a big draw and the giant Welshman 'singing': 'Buy some weed, hash or dope/Roll a joint and take a toke/Draw deeply on the smoke/And let your mind go…'

It's not hard to imagine that the hard rockers of music would always be up for a smoke, but in recent years even squeaky-clean teen bands such as S Club 7, Boyzone and Hear'Say have been caught tokin' or have called for the legalization of weed. Not forgetting, of course, Joseph 'Afroman' Foreman's worldwide smash and UK Number One 'Because I Got High' in 2001. Despite its humorously anti-grass lyrics, it was embraced equally by the establishment and stoners as being both anti- and pro-marijuana. Afroman even co-presented MTV's *Cannabis Night* in the

Left: Cannabis campaigner and Jamiroquai front man, Jay Kay.

UK in 2002, with viewers invited to vote for the Top 10 Stoner Videos. As Bob Dylan sang, 'The times, they are a-changin''.

'A few herbs and a bit of Benson...'

The Streets' groundbreaking 2002 *Original Pirate Material* album is littered with marijuana references as part of UK youth's everyday lives. 'Too Much Brandy' recounts a drugs excursion to Amsterdam's numerous coffee shops, and opens: 'Smell a good earth/The herbs make my nerves shudder/But where were you that cold December?/'Cos we were in the Grasshopper.' The pro-pot/anti-alcohol single 'The Irony of It All' cleverly juxtaposes the two experiences of Terry – a lager lout and 'upstanding citizen' – and Tim – a student and 'criminal', who 'in the eyes of society needs to be in jail for the choice of herbs I inhale'. As the song progresses Terry becomes increasingly obnoxious, drunk and incomprehensible, while Tim makes an excellent case for legalization.

Lastly, one could hardly not mention the appropriately named Mindless Drug Hoover and their own 'The Reefer Song' from 1993. The folksy track has become something of a stoner anthem in the UK and tells of our hero, who gets busted while smoking a spliff and having a bike ride. The rousing chorus goes: 'It's a reefer, do you want some, policeman?/It's a reefer, do you want a blast?/It's a reefer, do you want some, policeman?/Or would you prefer me to shove it up your arse?' He ends up

Above: Afroman would have written a caption here, but he got high.

in the police station with unexpected results: 'Well, I sold them two ounces and one sixteenth/And they rolled the biggest joint that the world has ever seen!'

Chapter 3

The Stoner's Guide to Smoking Accessories

Every true stoner knows that smoking a joint isn't just a case of throwing grass into a rolling paper and lighting it. There's the ritual. Fortunately there's a galaxy of gadgets to make life easier.

ROK-IT *(right)*
BONGS COME IN EVERY SIZE, SHAPE AND MATERIAL. THIS CLASSIC, IN CHROME AND GLASS, IS TOP OF THE RANGE. IT SEPARATES THE SMOKE OUT THROUGH A 14-PORT FILTRATION SYSTEM TO CREATE A COOL, SMOOTH BLAST OF INTOXICATING SMOKE. IT WORKS BY SEPARATING THE SMOKE THREE TIMES, SPLITTING IT INTO THOUSANDS OF TINY BUBBLES. THIS BABY'S EXPENSIVE, BUT IT'S WORTH IT. NOT FOR BEGINNERS.

ROOR ICEMASTER *(far right)*
CREATED BY GERMAN MARTIN BIRZL, THE ICEMASTER HAS NOTCHES FOR ICE CUBES TO BE DROPPED IN, CREATING A COOLER SMOKE THAT'S EASIER ON THE LUNGS. THE ROOR RANGE IS MADE FROM INCREDIBLY STRONG BORO SILICATE GLASS.

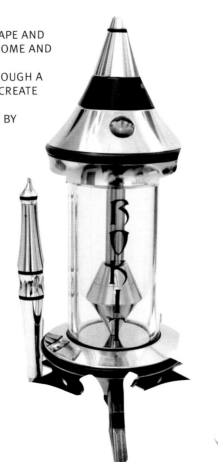

● It's important to clean out and maintain your bong, and replace gauzes in the hash bowl, in order to maintain its effectiveness.

SHERLOCK WATER PIPE *(below)*

THIS MINI 'BUBBLER' IS PART BONG/PART PIPE AND IS HAND-BLOWN. AS SUCH, ITS DESIGN IS COMPLETELY UNIQUE AND NO TWO PIPES ARE THE SAME. WHILE EXTREMELY BEAUTIFUL TO LOOK AT THEY CAN BE TRICKY TO CLEAN. THESE 'POCKET BONGS' ARE HANDY FOR THE TRAVELLING STONER AS A FULL LENGTH ONE IS AWKWARD TO CARRY AND COULD ATTRACT UNWANTED ATTENTION!

GECKO GLASS BONG *(above)*

THIS ELEGANT WORK OF ART MAKES A GREAT CONVERSATION PIECE STANDING A FOOT AND A HALF TALL (45CM)! GLASS BLOWN BONGS ALLOW FOR UNLIMITED CREATIVE DESIGNS FROM DOLPHINS TO DRAGONS.

METAL 'EXHAUST' BONG *(right)*

FOR THAT MORE MODERN, LESS HIPPIE, LOOK CHROME IS WHERE IT'S AT. THIS BACHELOR SPECIAL LOOKS SLICK AND MAKES SMOKE TASTE THE SAME. THE ADVANTAGE OF A BONG LIKE THIS IS THAT IT CAN BE HELD IN ONE HAND. IT'S CHEAP, IT'S STURDY AND IS EASILY DISASSEMBLED FOR CLEANING. AND IT COMES IN MANY COLOURS, LIKE YOUR TRIP.

CHEECH & CHONG BONG *(right)*

THE DOPE-HEAD DEMI-GODS FINALLY GAINED THE ICONIC STATUS THEY DESERVED WITH THIS CERAMIC BONG IN THE STYLE OF THE ANCIENT MAYANS. CHEECH MARIN HOLDS ALOFT THE HASH BOWL AS YOU LIGHT AND TAKE A TOKE FROM TOMMY CHONG'S ENORMOUS JOINT. THEN LAY BACK AND QUOTE YOUR FAVOURITE LINES... 'DAVE'S NOT HERE, MAN...'

THE TOWER OF POWER *(left)*

BONGS CAN BE MADE OUT OF PRACTICALLY ANYTHING (APPLES, MELONS, ETC.) SO WHY NOT ACRYLIC? THIS ARCHITECTURALLY ARRESTING CREATION HAS THREE CHAMBERS AND THE SMOKE PASSES THROUGH THE NUMEROUS PIPES, COOLING ALL THE WAY TO THE TOP. SWEET.

CERAMIC GUN BONG *(above)*

IF YOU'RE GOING TO BLOW YOUR BRAINS OUT, DO IT IN STYLE! THE CERAMIC NATURALLY CREATES A SMOOTH SMOKE SO ALL YOU HAVE TO DO IS PUT THE BARREL IN YOUR MOUTH AND SQUEEZE THE TRIGGER.

THE METEORITE HOOKAH *(below)*

THE MORE TRADITIONAL HOOKAH, OR SHISHA, STYLE BONGS ORIGINATED IN THE 16TH CENTURY AND WERE ORIGINALLY MADE FROM COCONUT SHELLS AND BAMBOO. 100 YEARS LATER THEY SPREAD ACROSS THE ARAB WORLD WHERE CRAFTSMEN TRADED COCONUTS FOR GLASS AND BAMBOO FOR METAL.

BAMBOO BONG *(right)*

THIS PARTICULAR STYLE OF BONG ORIGINATED IN THE FAR EAST, WITH LOCALS HOLLOWING OUT LARGE BAMBOO SHOOTS TO CREATE A SMOKE CHAMBER IN ORDER TO GET A GREATER HIGH. SIMPLE, BUT EFFECTIVE. THEY PROVED VERY POPULAR WITH AMERICAN G.I.s DURING THE VIETNAM WAR. CHARLIE MIGHT NOT SURF, BUT HE KNOWS HOW TO SMOKE!

TWO-MAN SMILEY *(left)*

WHY WAIT FOR YOUR FRIEND TO FINISH TOKING BEFORE PASSING IT ROUND? WITH MODERN BONGS YOU CAN GET STONED TOGETHER AND SHARE THE SAME HIGH! AND WHAT BETTER WAY THAN USING THAT ICONIC SYMBOL OF THE SECOND SUMMER OF LOVE, THE SMILEY FACE. FOR A SWEETER FLAVOUR TRY USING WINE INSTEAD OF WATER.

FOUR-MAN ALIEN BONG *(right)*

HAVING A PARTY? THEN THIS BABY'S FOR YOU! FOUR TOKERS CAN SHARE THE CONTENTS OF THIS ALIEN BRAIN. DIFFERENT LIQUIDS CAN FLAVOUR THE SMOKE AND IT CAN BE FUN EXPERIMENTING WITH JUICES LIKE ORANGE AND LEMON FOR A ZESTY ZING TO YOUR HIGH. FEED YOUR HEAD!

FOUR-PIECE HOOKAH *(right)*

THIS MORE TRADITIONAL FOUR-SHARE HOOKAH IS BY NO MEANS LESS EFFECTIVE. THERE ARE APPROXIMATELY OVER A BILLION HOOKAH, OR 'HUBBLY-BUBBLY' SMOKERS IN THE WORLD TODAY, ALTHOUGH MANY USE THEM SIMPLY TO SMOKE APPLE- OR CITRUS-FLAVOURED TOBACCO, RATHER THAN DOPE.

SWEETLEAF WOODEN GRINDER *(above)*

OFTEN BUDS AND FLOWER HEADS CAN BE DRIED QUITE COMPACT AND HARD TO BREAK UP TO SPRINKLE IN A JOINT. HERE'S WHERE GRINDERS COME INTO THEIR OWN. JUST DROP YOUR STASH IN, GIVE IT A TWIST AND BINGO! SMALL PIECES, PERFECT FOR PUFFING.

PIECEMAKER POLLEN PRESSER *(right)*

THIS MARVELLOUS PIECE OF KIT COMPRESSES THE BELOVED POLLEN OF THE PLANT INTO A HANDY SOLID BLOCK. YOU CAN EVEN GET CUSTOMIZED DISCS TO EMBOSS YOUR OWN LOGO!

POLLEN HERB GRINDER *(below)*

THIS 'KING OF GRINDERS' NOT ONLY BREAKS UP GRASS BUT IT PRACTICALLY VAPORIZES IT SO THAT THE PRECIOUS CRYSTALS CONTAINING THE ALL-IMPORTANT THC ACTIVE INGREDIENT ARE COLLECTED IN SEVERAL CHAMBERS BELOW. ONCE ENOUGH CRYSTALS ARE COLLECTED THEY CAN BE PRESSED TOGETHER AND SMOKED FOR ONE OF THE PUREST HIGHS.

● Pollen has a much higher content of tetrahydrocannabinol, the active ingredient that gives smokers that buzz, hence it is valued highly.

EASYLEAF HASH GRINDER *(right)*

GRINDERS ARE NOT JUST FOR GRASS. THIS HEAVY-DUTY METAL MONSTER IS MORE THAN CAPABLE OF GRINDING UP PRIME MOROCCAN KETAMA HASHISH. GRINDING HASH MEANS YOU DON'T HAVE TO BURN IT TO SOFTEN IT FOR FLAKING OFF INTO YOUR JOINT, WHICH IN TURN MEANS YOU'RE NOT WASTING ANY BEFORE YOU GET TO SMOKE IT!

● This gadget is perfect for grating and sprinkling nutmeg and hash on the cannabis cocktails on page 196.

GRATER *(left)*

A SIMPLER, CHEAPER ALTERNATIVE TO GRINDING HASH IS TO USE THIS MINI POCKET-SIZED GRATER, WHICH ALSO ACTS AS A HANDY ROLLING PAPER HOLDER.

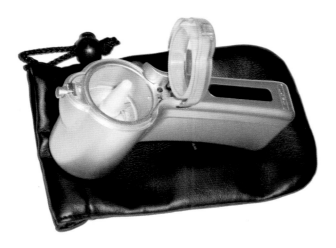

ELECTRIC HERB GRINDER MAX *(left)*

BATTERY-POWERED GRINDERS ARE JUST ONE OF MANY OF THE LATEST GIZMOS IN THE MODERN-DAY STONER'S ARSENAL. NOT ONLY DOES THIS STAINLESS STEEL BABY TAKE THE EFFORT OUT OF GRINDING ON THOSE DAYS WHEN YOU'RE JUST TOO WASTED, BUT IT LIGHTS UP WHEN IN USE. COOL!

ELECTRIC HERB GRINDER *(right)*

NOT QUITE AS POWERFUL AS ITS BIG BROTHER, THIS HELPFUL TOOL STILL WORKS WONDERS. SIMPLY SLAP IN THE HERBS, FLICK THE SWITCH AND WATCH IT DO THE WORK FOR YOU. .

SIX-SHOOTER PIPE *(below)*
LOAD THIS BEAUTY UP WITH SIX BLASTS OF HASH TO SAVE YOU TIME LATER AND SHARE THE WEALTH AMONG FIVE FRIENDS. OR YOU COULD BE TOTALLY GREEDY AND BOGART THE ENTIRE PIPE AND EVEN FILL ONE CHAMBER UP WITH DRIED MUD AND PLAY RUSSIAN ROULETTE! SIMPLY TOKE AND TWIST.

• Crap at rolling joints? Bongs too big to take out with you? What you need is a pipe! Small, convenient and a pure smoke.

SIX SPIRAL GLASS PIPE *(right)*
THESE CHIC LITTLE PIPES COME IN THEIR OWN PRESENTATION BOX AND ARE AVAILABLE IN FOUR, SIX AND EVEN EIGHT SPIRALS. THE MORE SPIRALS THERE ARE THE COOLER THE SMOKE IS. HOWEVER, TO KEEP THESE BEAUTIES LOOKING GOOD YOU'LL NEED TO INVEST IN SOME PIPECLEANERS. THE ADVANTAGE OF A PIPE IS THAT THERE'S NO NEED FOR TOBACCO.

COLOURED GLASS PIPE *(bottom)*

THIS STYLISH LITTLE NUMBER IS SIMPLE TO CLEAN. PIPES CLOG UP EASILY BECAUSE WHEN THE HASH BURNS A SMALL PERCENTAGE MELTS AND FORMS HASH OIL, BLOCKING THE GAUZE. THEREFORE, WHILE CLEANING OUT PIPES REGULARLY HELPS, YOU WILL NEED TO REPLACE THE GAUZES AS WELL.

WOODEN PIPE *(below)*

THIS DISCRETE WOODEN PIPE HAS A LARGE BOWL SO IT CAN BE PACKED WITH HERBS OR HASH FOR A SERIOUS MASH-UP. LIKE MOST PIPES, IT SHOULD BE USED WITH A GAUZE.

PURPLE METAL PIPE *(below right)*

THIS SIMPLE, YET STYLISH, PIPE IS MADE FROM ANODIZED
METAL SO IT WON'T RUST OR TARNISH EASILY. PIPES ARE
POPULAR, PARTICULARLY IN JAPAN, AS THEY ARE PORTABLE
AND CAN BE CONCEALED QUICKLY WITH MINIMUM FUSS
SHOULD THE OLD BILL COME SNOOPING AROUND.

● Sometimes you can
have too much of a
good thing and the
choice of pipes
available can be
overwhelming!

MANGO WOOD PIPE *(below left)*

THIS SENSUOUS THAI-BASED DESIGN IS
MADE FROM THE MANGO TREE (MANGIFERA
INDICA). MANGO IS A BLONDE HARD WOOD, WHICH
MEANS THE PIPE IS BEAUTIFUL AND YET SHOULD
LAST A LONG TIME.

RED MUSHROOM PIPE *(right)*

WHEN DISCRETION IS THE BETTER PART OF GETTING STONED, THIS HANDY KEY CHAIN COMES APART AND REFORMS AS A NEAT, PORTABLE METAL PIPE. HOWEVER, ANYONE WITH A SLIGHT KNOWLEDGE OF PLANTS WOULD SPOT THAT IT IS IN THE SHAPE OF A PSILOCYBIN OR MAGIC MUSHROOM, WHICH MIGHT GIVE THE GAME AWAY!

SIX-HIT METAL PIPE *(left)*

ANOTHER SIX-CHAMBER SPECIAL, BUT THIS ONE CAN BE BROKEN DOWN FOR EASY CARRYING. ANOTHER METAL PIPE IS THE CLEVER FOLD-A-BOWL WHICH PACKS FLAT, IN ELEVEN MOVES, TO A CREDIT CARD SIZE SO IT CAN BE CARRIED IN A WALLET OR PURSE. YOU NEED NEVER BE CAUGHT SHORT AGAIN WITHOUT A PIPE!

EBONY TOWER *(below)*

THIS PIECE OF INSPIRED DESIGN ALLOWS A TOKER TO SMOKE THREE WAYS; AS A SMALL TRAVELLING PIPE, AS A CHILLUM, OR AS A LARGE TOWER PIPE FOR THAT EXTRA PUNCH. THE WHOLE KIT DISMANTLES AND CAN BE CARRIED NEATLY IN A POCKET. THREE TIMES THE FUN!

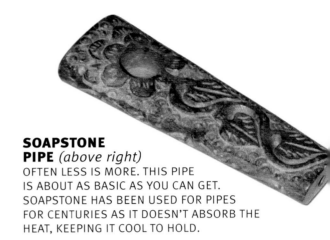

SOAPSTONE PIPE *(above right)*

OFTEN LESS IS MORE. THIS PIPE IS ABOUT AS BASIC AS YOU CAN GET. SOAPSTONE HAS BEEN USED FOR PIPES FOR CENTURIES AS IT DOESN'T ABSORB THE HEAT, KEEPING IT COOL TO HOLD.

FIMO PIPE LEAF DESIGN *(below)*

WITH THIS COLOURFUL CLAY, SIMPLE, EYE-CATCHING PIPES CAN BE MADE IN A WHOLE ARRAY OF DESIGNS THAT HAVE A PLEASANT SILICONE FEEL. THE PERFECT 'DISPOSABLE' PIPE FOR THE BEACH.

KING AMAZED, GUNMETAL GREY *(above)*

THIS GIANT OF A PIPE (15CM/6 IN LONG) HOLDS A MASSIVE 275 GRAMS (10OZ) OF CHOICE SILVER HAZE, OR WHATEVER YOUR PREFERRED SMOKE IS. ITS DEEPER SMOKE PATH, THROUGH A COOLING MAZE-LIKE STRUCTURE, ENSURES IT'S EASY ON THE LUNGS.

• Pipes come in many designs these days, many of them sculpted into miniature works of art. Appearances can be deceptive!

BUL-IT *(below)*

THE ONLY TIME WHEN BITING THE BULLET ISN'T A BAD THING! THIS CHEEKY LITTLE PIPE DOES A SIMILAR JOB AS THE 'KING AMAZED', IN A STYLISH DESIGN. AVAILABLE IN EITHER CHROME OR BRASS IT'S A HIGH-CALIBRE HIT THAT'S GUARANTEED TO BLOW YOUR HEAD CLEAN OFF YOUR SHOULDERS!

LARGE BATTERY PIPE *(right)*

OK, SO YOU MAY BE TOO MONGED TO ROLL A JOINT, BUT NOW YOU DON'T EVEN HAVE TO INHALE THANKS TO THIS LITTLE BEAUTY. THE BUILT-IN FAN COOLS THE SMOKE AND GENTLY BLOWS IT INTO THE MOUTH OF THE UNCONSCIOUS SMOKER WHO WANTS TO MAINTAIN THEIR HIGH! AS ONE USER PUT IT, 'GOOD FOR CHILL SMOKING.'

• Both these labour saving devices are perfect for the stoner who doesn't have to try...too hard!

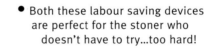

THE BUKKET *(left)*

THIS INGENIOUS GRAVITY BONG WITH AN ACCORDION LUNG FILLS UP WITH SMOKE AND THEN COMPRESSES WHEN INHALED. BUT IT CAN PROVE TOO POPULAR ACCORDING TO ONE FAN, 'AN UNCLE OF MINE IS NOT TOO FAR FROM GOING INTO A CONSTANT COMATOSE STATE NOW... LOOKS LIKE A TOY BUT IT AIN'T!'

ROYAL BLUNTS, COGNAC AND HONEY *(right)*

A FAVOURITE WITH THE HIP-HOP CROWD, BLUNTS ARE MADE FROM ROLLING A JOINT INSIDE A TOBACCO LEAF. THE LEAVES ARE MARINATED IN VARIOUS FLAVOURS FOR THAT EXTRA DELUXE SMOKE. BIG, BAD AND A BLAST, THAT'S THE BLUNT!

BOB MARLEY ROACH PAPERS *(left)*

RASTAFARIAN REGGAE ROYALTY ON A ROACH! ROACHES ARE ESSENTIAL FOR KEEPING THE END OF A JOINT OPEN AND CLEAR TO ALLOW THE SMOKE TO FLOW FREELY (THERE'S NOTHING WORSE THAN A SOGGY, CLOSED-UP JOINT YOU CAN'T GET A HIT FROM). YOU CAN MAKE A ROACH FROM ANY PIECE OF SMALL CARD TORN UP (SUCH AS A ROLLING PAPER PACKET), BUT FOR THE TRUE AFICIONADO THESE LITTLE BOOKS ARE ESSENTIAL.

HEMP RIPS *(left)*

RIPS ROCK SIMPLY BECAUSE UNLIKE MANY PAPERS, YOU CAN TEAR OFF AS MUCH OR AS LITTLE AS YOU NEED. THE GUM IS MADE FROM A SLOW-BURNING VEGETABLE MATERIAL TO ALLOW FOR A LONGER SMOKE. ADD TO THIS THE FACT THESE PAPERS ARE ACTUALLY MADE FROM 100% HEMP AND YOU'RE MAKING A POLITICAL STATEMENT AS WELL!

• Nearly all paper manufacturers deny their products are for smoking weed. Yeah, right.

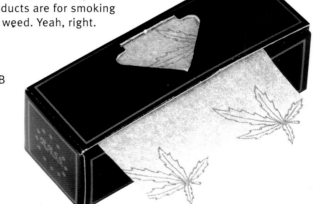

RASS LEAF PAPERS *(right)*

PAPERS ARE THE MOST POPULAR WAY OF SMOKING THE HEALING HERB AND ARE ESSENTIAL FOR THOSE WITHOUT A PIPE OR BONG, WHO WANT TO ROLL EITHER A 'NEW YORK JOINT' TOOTHPICK FOR PERSONAL USE, OR A MASSIVE 'CAMBERWELL CARROT' TO SHARE WITH FRIENDS. AFICIONADOS ALSO COLLECT RARE PAPERS FROM THE SIXTIES AND SEVENTIES.

FLAVOURED PAPERS, GRAPE *(below)*

TO ADD A TOUCH OF FLAVOUR TO YOUR SMOKE WHY NOT TRY A
FLAVOURED PAPER, SUCH AS WATERMELON, VANILLA, BANANA,
COCONUT OR GRAPE? NOT ONLY DO THEY FLAVOUR THE SMOKE,
BUT THEY LEAVE A LOVELY, SWEET TASTE ON THE LIPS AS WELL.

STONE CHILLUM *(right)*

THESE UNIQUE 'PIPES' HAVE A SMALL
STONE INSIDE, PREVENTING THE
HASH/TOBACCO MIX FROM DROPPING
THROUGH. THE TRICK OF SMOKING A
CHILLUM IS TO CREATE A CHAMBER BY
CUPPING YOUR HANDS UNDERNEATH AND
INHALING THE SMOKE FROM THERE. THIS
MEANS YOU OFTEN NEED A BUDDY TO
HELP SPARK YOU UP.

• Chillums
traditionally come
from India and are
used by holy men,
or sadhus, for
smoking a
hash/tobacco mix
as a sacred
sacrament.

89

VAPIR AIR-TWO DIGITAL AIR VAPORIZER CITRUS *(below)*
THIS IS THE CUTTING EDGE OF 21ST CENTURY SMOKING. THE VAPIR INSTANTLY TURNS HASH OR HERBAL MIXES INTO AN AEROSOL-LIKE VAPOUR FOR EASY INHALATION AND THE TEMPERATURE IS DIGITALLY CONTROLLED. THE ONLY THING IT DOESN'T DO IS MAKE TOAST.

• Vaporizers are the healthiest way of smoking cannabis as they release the psychoactive cannabinoids in vapor without burning the plant material.

VAPORTEC VAPORIZER *(above)*
THE DADDY OF ALL MODERN VAPOUR TECHNOLOGY, THIS MIRACLE MACHINE TURNS THE ACTIVE THC CONTENT INTO A VAPOR THUS RELEASING THE HIGH, BUT NOT THE UNWANTED TAR CAUSED BY BURNING THE PLANT FIBRE, CREATING A PURE SMOKE.

VOLCANO VAPORIZER *(below left)*

THE ULTIMATE PARTY PIECE AND 2003 CANNABIS CUP WINNER, THIS FUN DEVICE VAPORIZES THE HASH OR GRASS AND FILLS A BAG WITH PURE VAPOUR. THE BAG IS THEN PASSED AROUND AND SMOKED, GIVING BETWEEN TWO AND SIX HITS.

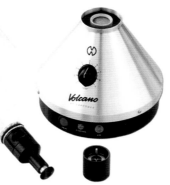

BLUE MEANIE VAPORIZER *(right)*

ONE OF THE ORIGINAL VAPORIZERS TO BE MARKETED, THE BLUE MEANIE IS CHEAPER THAN MANY OF THE OTHERS, BUT IS STILL HIGHLY EFFECTIVE AND RELIABLE.

CANNABIS FLAVOURED
LOLLIES *(below)*

IF YOU GET THE MUNCHIES ENJOY THESE
SWEETS OR SOME INDICA FLOWER CHEWING
GUM, NATURALLY FLAVOURED WITH SWISS
CANNABIS FLOWERS, CARDAMOM AND
CINNAMON. AND DON'T FORGET A SIP
OR TWO OF HEMP CHAMPAGNE
OR BEER TO WASH IT DOWN
WITH AFTERWARDS.

TWO-OUNCE TIN,
SUPER SKUNK *(right)*

IT'S ALL VERY WELL SMOKING
GRASS, BUT WHERE DO YOU KEEP
YOUR STASH? THE ANSWER IS, OF
COURSE, A TOBACCO TIN. A LARGE
ONE WILL NOT ONLY HOLD
EVERYTHING YOU NEED: YOUR SKINS,
LIGHTER, ROACH PAPERS, ETC., BUT IT
WILL ALSO KEEP ANY TOBACCO OR
GRASS MOIST AND FRESH. THE
PERFECT STONER'S SURVIVAL KIT.

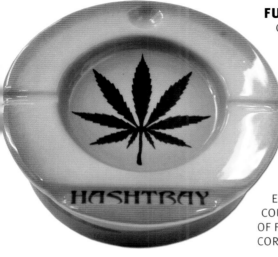

FUNKY AS FUK ASHTRAY *(left)*

OF COURSE THERE'S THE DOWNER OF YOUR SMOKING BY-PRODUCT, AND WHERE ELSE SHOULD IT GO BUT IN THESE COOL 'HASH-TRAYS'. EACH ONE IS HAND-PAINTED AND FIRED IN A KILN AND COMES WITH A ROLLING GROOVE TO AID SKINNING UP.

GSUB METAL ROLLING TRAY *(below)*

WHAT DO YOU GET THE STONER WHO HAS EVERYTHING? THEIR OWN 'WORKSTATION' OF COURSE! HERE EVERYTHING'S BEEN THOUGHT OF FROM THE ROLLING GROOVE AND BUDS CORNER TO A PAPER STASH.

• Once you've bought all your gear, it's time to get your other gear out and get rolling. Happy trails!

Chapter 4

Top 50 Greatest Potheads

Millions of stoners enjoy a puff around the world so why should famous people be any different? Whether to escape the stress of fame or to boost their creativity, there are some figures who will be inextricably linked with ganja.

Top 50 Greatest Potheads

This gathering of the obvious and the unlikely jokers, smokers and midnight tokers are all listed here as they have furthered the cause of the weed. Whether they have been at the forefront of the legalization lobby, such as Country and Western singer Willie Nelson and director Robert Altman, or have been simply caught with a fat doobie on their lips, they've all enjoyed a reefer from time to time.

Marijuana musicians

Shaun Ryder

It's a miracle this man is still alive. The Mancunian former lead singer of the Happy Mondays and Black Grape is as famous for the huge quantities of drugs he's taken as he is for his musical abilities. 'I'm not going to turn around and start telling every little fucker to start smoking pot… but when I started smoking pot and dropping trips I wanted to get involved in how things work.' Over the years Ryder has taken almost every conceivable prescription and street drug known to man, including Temazipan, cocaine, Ecstasy, LSD and heroin. Now reformed, he just enjoys the odd bit of Skunk: 'When I'm at home with my family I have a few lagers, smoke a bit of weed, and that's it.'

Bing Crosby *(above)*
The king of croon maintained his mellow demeanour thanks to a few tokes on the herb.

Crosby started singing jazz during the 1920s and was switched on to reefer by jazz great Louis Armstrong. The ganja-loving Armstrong appeared in several movies with Crosby, and they teamed up on the 1951 hit single 'Gone Fishin'. Bing's oldest son, Gary, described how his father told him he should just smoke pot instead of over-drinking, and claimed that dope affected his father's casual musical and theatrical style. 'If you look at the way he sang and the way he walked and talked,' said Gary, 'you could make a pretty good case for somebody who was loaded.'

David Ford interviewed Crosby in 1962 and asked him whether 'at home you might put a little grass in your famous pipe?' Ford recounted: 'He looked me right in the eyes and rewarded me with a generous grin and a wink. I've had various musicians tell me that in fact he smoked a lot of pot, and that it did keep him mellow.'

In numerous interviews during the Sixties and Seventies Crosby clearly stated he thought Mary Jane should be legal, or at least be decriminalized. Bing passed on to the happy hemping grounds in 1978 after a heart attack.

S Club 7
… or rather the S Club 3 boys. Jon Lee, Paul Cattermole and Bradley McIntosh were busted in Covent Garden, London, for possession of cannabis in 2001. This was a shock revelation for the squeaky-clean pop band's pre-teen fans, and the boys apologized for being 'stupid' – presumably stupid for being caught. Cynics suggested the whole stunt was organized by their manager, Simon Fuller, the man behind the Spice Girls. Still, with the sweet smell of grass in the air, truly, 'there ain't no party like an S Club party'. But all parties eventually have to end, and the band split in 2003.

Willie Nelson *(above)*

The tax-dodging country singer and actor is perhaps one of the most vocal and unexpected pro-marijuana voices in America. He told Country Music Television's Inside Fame programme, 'I used to smoke three, four packs of cigarettes a day. I used to drink as much whisky and beer as anybody in the world. I would have been dead if it hadn't been for pot, because when I started smoking pot I quit smoking cigarettes and drinking.' Nelson later stated, 'I think people need to be educated to the fact that marijuana is not a drug. Marijuana is an herb and a flower. God put it here. If He put it here

nd He wants it to grow, what gives the
overnment the right to say that God is wrong?'
Jelson was busted in Texas in 1995 with pot in
is car, but charges were dropped later when the
earch was deemed illegal. He is currently on the
dvisory board of the National Organisation for
ne Reform of Marijuana Laws (NORML), the
on-profit group promoting legalization of
narijuana.

Whitney Houston

anuary 2000 wasn't a good month for the diva
vhen she was searched by Hawaiian airport
ecurity guards. They discovered 15g ($^1/_2$ oz) of
ot in her carry-on bag, although the charges
vere later dropped. In 2002, she admitted on
elevision to abusing cocaine, marijuana and
arious other drugs, but she claimed to have
topped using illegal drugs. However, her
omment, 'Crack is cheap. I make too much
noney to ever smoke crack – let's get that
traight. OK?' caused a new uproar. Pot-smoking
ins in Houston's family, as her singer cousin,
)ionne Warwick, 63, was also arrested at
'liami airport in 2002 for possession of
narijuana cigarettes.

Art Garfunkel *(top right)*

Vhen John Lennon was almost kicked out of the
SA in the Seventies, Garfunkel famously said,
f John Lennon is deported, I'm leaving too...
vith my musicians... and my marijuana.'
Infortunately his marijuana got the singer

arrested in January 2004. Still tokin' after all
these years, the 62-year-old former member of
the duo Simon and Garfunkel was riding in the
back of a limo when a state trooper pulled the
driver over for speeding and noticed the scent of
dope coming from the back of the limo. The
policeman discovered a small amount of pot in
Garfunkel's jacket pocket, and the singer was
forced to pay a $200 fine.

Mick Jagger

The rubber-lipped rock star was introduced to
the wacky baccy in 1966 by Paul McCartney,
who was turned onto it by Bob Dylan. The

Above: The 1967 Rolling Stones bust sparked off a media frenzy that turned Mick Jagger and Keith Richard into cause Celebs.

following year Jagger was busted in an infamous police raid on Keith Richard's house, Redlands, in West Sussex. The tabloids went into a frenzy, referring to 'Miss X' – stark naked under a fur rug and allegedly under the influence of marijuana. At the trial the judge told the jury to disregard Marianne Faithfull's evidence that she hadn't been smoking pot at the time. Richard was sentenced to a year in prison, plus £500 costs,

simply for allowing his house to be used as a venue for smoking 'Indian hemp'. Jagger, however, was given three months for possessing four pep pills that had been bought legally in Italy. This injustice prompted *The Times* to comment 'Who breaks a butterfly on a wheel?' In fact the only person found in possession of cannabis at Redlands was a Canadian drug dealer called David Scheidermann, who vanished and who Keith Richard denounced as a *News of the World* informer. On appeal Richard's case was quashed and Jagger was let off with a conditional discharge.

Paul McCartney

McCartney, along with the rest of The Beatles, was turned on to the herb by Bob Dylan in 1964. 'We were kind of proud to have been introduced to pot by Dylan,' said McCartney. 'That was rather a coup. It was like being introduced to meditation and given your mantra by Maharishi.

There was a certain status to it...' Three years later he helped pay for an advertisement in *The Times* that called for legalization of pot possession, release of all prisoners on possession

Below: Paul McCartney being arrested by the police at Tokyo International Airport.

charges and government research into marijuana's medical uses. 'I think we could decriminalize marijuana, and I'd like to see a really unbiased medical report on it,' he said after being deported from Japan in 1980 for bringing nearly 200g (7oz) of marijuana into Tokyo during Wings' Band on the Run tour. Paul's wife and band member, Linda, made headlines with her open fondness for marijuana. She smoked pot to ease the discomfort of chemotherapy while suffering from breast cancer. She died in 1998.

Louis Armstrong (left)

The jazz player introduced his mutual friends Blow and Bing [Crosby] to each other. Old Satchmo was busted in 1931 for possession of 'Tea', as it was called back then – and received a suspended sentence. 'It really puzzles me to see marijuana connected with narcotics… dope and all that crap. It's a thousand times better than whisky – it's an assistant – a friend.' Armstrong's main dealer was the jazz clarinettist Milton 'Mezz' Mezzrow, a man more famous for his marijuana than his music. So much so that the name 'mezz' became synonymous for a fat joint.

Bob Marley (above right)

The Rastafarian musician was single-handedly responsible for bringing reggae out of Jamaica and to a mainstream audience. His vast body of work embraced everything from ska to rock steady to reggae while using music as a social force with universal appeal.

The teenage Marley formed a trio in 1963 with friends Neville 'Bunny' O'Riley Livingston (later Bunny Wailer) and Peter McIntosh (later Peter Tosh). As practising Rastas, they grew their hair in dreadlocks and smoked marijuana, believing it to be a sacred herb that brought enlightenment.

103

"When you return to this mundane sphere from your visionary world, you would seem to leave a Neapolitan spring for a Lapland winter – to quit paradise for earth – heaven for hell! Taste the hashish, guest of mine – taste the hashish!"

Alexander Dumas, The Count of Monte Cristo

beyond their native Jamaican home base. The song tells the story of a feud between an overzealous sheriff and a ganja farmer in Jamaica: 'Sheriff John Brown always hate I/For what, I never know/Every time I plant a seed/He say, kill it before it grow/He said, kill them before they grow.'

So influential a cultural icon had Marley become on his home island by the mid-Seventies that *Time* magazine announced, 'He rivals the government as a political force.' Marley died aged 36 of cancer in 1981, and was buried in Jamaica with full state honours. Today his legacy lives on with sales of *Legend* (a best-of compilation spanning 1972–81) topping 10 million copies in the USA alone, making it the best-selling reggae album in history.

Snoop Dogg *(left)*

Rapper Calvin Broadus was nicknamed 'Snoopy' by his mother, so he took the stage name Snoop Doggy Dogg or Snoop Dogg. He was frequently in trouble with drugs and the law as a young man, and was in and out of jail for three years. Dogg built his career on cannabis, with most of his music and movie output being based upon pot culture references. He collaborated with Dr Dre (see Maui Wowie Music chapter) on Dre's debut dope-inspired album, *The Chronic*. Dogg's *Doggystyle* (1993), became the first debut album ever to enter the charts at No. 1, helping to fuel the rise of West Coast gangsta rap.

Dogg has been busted a few times, including in 2001, when Ohio State Troopers searched his tour bus and found about 200g (7oz) of bud. The raid happened while Snoop was travelling with his Puff, Puff, Pass tour – named after the correct etiquette for sharing a joint. He was named 'Stoner of the Year, 2002' by *High Times* magazine, but that year he announced that he was giving up drinking and drugs. 'Drugs cloud your vision,' Dogg told the media. 'I was having fun when I was getting high. Don't regret none of the times I was on it... [But] I said "Let me stop smoking dope so I can get a better vision of myself, see who I am and what I mean to the world. What I mean to my kids and what I mean to life in general."'

Dogg later admitted doing anti-drug ads while getting high himself. 'I used to do public service announcements and tell the kids, "Say no to drugs", and [I was] high as fuck – very hypocritical.'

Gene Krupa

The superb drummer smoked but wasn't a huge a fan of the green, unlike many of his jazz contemporaries. But unfortunately for Krupa, while in San Francisco in the summer of 1943 he was followed by narcotics officers. A friend had bought him some grass as a present. 'The ridiculous thing was that I was such a boozer I never thought about grass,' recalled Krupa. 'I'd take grass and it would put me to sleep. I was an out-and-out lush.' The Feds arrested him and

Bob Dylan *(left)*

Dylan was born Robert Allen Zimmerman in 1941 in Duluth, Minnesota, in the USA, and is generally regarded as one of America's greatest popular songwriters alongside Irving Berlin, Woody Guthrie and Hank Williams. His 1965 'Mr Tambourine Man' was about a drugs comedown and was implicitly infused with pot consciousness. The following year, 'Rainy Day Women#12 & 35', the opening track from his *Blonde On Blonde* album, was an instant success, reaching No. 2. This was despite it being banned from the radio because of its explicit marijuana lyrics: 'I would not feel so alone/Everybody must get stoned'. Dylan was turned onto grass by friend and Beat poet, Allen Ginsberg. The singer, in turn, switched the Beatles onto the benefits of weed.

Chrissie Hynde

The lead singer and founder of the Pretenders was born in Akron, Ohio. She bought a one-way ticket to London, where she became a rock critic and founded her band. Hynde has never been afraid to voice her strong opinions on topics she believes in, from ending cruelty to animals to ending pot criminalization. In October 1997 she appeared on the cover of *High Times*, speaking on behalf of legalization. The following month, at a concert held on National Medical Marijuana Day, she and drummer Martin Chambers wore green ribbons onstage and Hynde stopped the show to announce that, 'We do endorse the use

charged Krupa with possession, and with 'contributing to the delinquency of a minor' – Krupa's valet at the time was 17-year-old John Pateakos. Krupa had sent Pateakos to get rid of the joints, but the valet was arrested before he could flush them. The FBI locked Krupa up for 84 days. Later the charges were dropped.

Reefer royalty and puffing politicians

Queen Victoria

Not an actual stoner as such, old Vic used to neck back bottles of cannabis tincture to help ease her savage period pains. Her physician, Sir J. Russell Reynolds, reported in the first issue of *The Lancet* in 1890, that he had been prescribing cannabis for 30 years and that he considered it 'one of the most valuable medicines we possess'. This typical use of marijuana for medicinal purposes surely had Her Royally High and most amused.

Prince Harry *(left)*

Third in line to the throne, the son of the Prince of Wales and Princess Di was busted in 2001, aged 16, when his old man (or rather a security officer) caught him having a few blasts in the shed round the back of his local pub. Prince Charles then took his son to a drug rehabilitation centre to see some heroin addicts to scare the crap out of Harry. Whether this worked is doubtful. The whole affair gave Harry extra street cred, and the media dubbed him 'Harry Pothead' after J.K. Rowling's famous wizard.

Jenna and Barbara Bush

President George W. Bush's wayward twin daughters have been a constant discomfiture to

of the herb for medical and other reasons. And I can tell you at forty-six that marijuana is the key to longevity.' Hynde now says she no longer tokes, but her song 'Legalize Me' remains an anthem for marijuana smokers.

109

him. The dynamic duo were outed as tokers by Ashton Kutcher, stoner star of *Dude, Where's My Car?*, in the May 2003 issue of *Rolling Stone*. 'The Bushes were underage-drinking at my house,' said Kutcher, describing a party in December 2001. 'When I checked outside, one of the Secret Service guys asked me if they'd be spending the night. I said no. And then I go upstairs to see another friend, and I can smell the green wafting out under his door. I open the door, and there he is smoking out the Bush twins on his hookah.' Apparently when Daddy Bush heard about the article he got on the phone to his toking twins. 'George told his daughters he remembers what it's like to be young and carefree,' a close source revealed. 'But he also explained it was more than a little embarrassing to read that his daughters were surrounded by clouds of marijuana smoke in a young Hollywood hunk's bedroom.' George W. himself is a reformed cokehead and alcoholic, 'when I was young and irresponsible' – as opposed to old and irresponsible now.

Bill Clinton *(left)*

The former US President studied at Oxford University in his youth, and while there 'I experimented with marijuana a time or two.' This caused a furore, and to counterbalance the outrage Clinton added weakly, 'I didn't like it. I didn't inhale.' This became a huge joke, to the point that American chat show host Jay Leno commented, 'Forty million Americans smoked marijuana; the only ones who didn't like it were Judge Ginsberg, Clarence Thomas and Bill Clinton.' Ironically, while in office Clinton actually stepped up the War on Drugs. It appears he really didn't like it.

Newt Gingrich

The US Congressman and Speaker of the House co-introduced legislation to allow marijuana's use as a medicine at the Federal level on 16 September 1981. Six months later he wrote in the *Journal of the American Medical Association*, 'We believe licensed physicians are competent to employ marijuana, and patients have a right to obtain marijuana legally, under medical supervision, from a regulated source… Federal policies do not reflect a factual or balanced assessment of marijuana's use as a medicate.' Gingrich confessed in 1995 in the *Economist* to smoking a few blunts when he was in college: 'That was a sign we were alive and in graduate school in that era [the 1970s]'. But his political double standards kicked in a year later, when he attacked Bill Clinton's press secretary Mike McCurry for making the same admission.

Whacked-out writers

William Shakespeare

In 2001 clay pipe fragments excavated from the blissed-out Bard's Stratford-upon-Avon home contained small amounts of cocaine and myristic

Above: "To toke, or not to toke, that is the question..." Britain's greatest playwright, Shakespeare was a serious stoner scribe.

acid – a hallucinogenic derived from plants, including nutmeg. The pipes also contained evidence of cannabis sativa, and use by Shakespeare is hinted in Sonnet 76, the 'noted weed' sonnet:

To new-found methods and to compounds strange?
Why write I still all one, ever the same,
And keep invention in a noted weed,
That every word doth almost tell my name,
Showing their birth, and where they did
proceed?

Other pot poetry includes Sonnet 27, where he talks of 'a journey in his head'.

Stephen King

The best-selling author told *High Times* magazine in 1980: 'I think that marijuana should not only be legal, I think it should be a cottage industry. It would be wonderful for the state of Maine. There's some pretty good home-grown dope. I'm sure it would be even better if you could grow it with fertilizers and have greenhouses...'

Many characters in his books smoke dope, including Darla Gaines in *TommyKnockers* and Bruce Trevor in *Carrie*. His 1996 book *Desperation* opens with the central characters being busted for inadvertently transporting a large bag of marijuana.

Will Self

The novelist and journalist certainly knows his drugs. The former junkie was caught doing heroin in 1997 on the Prime Minister's plane and was sacked from *The Observer* newspaper. 'The only thing that occurred to me – because I was smoking a lot of pot – was that I must stay downwind of the PM's Special Branch.' Being a

formed addict and now a game show regular,
e understandably has strong views on dope:
. Perhaps everyone could sit down and plan a
nsible, enforceable drug policy. One that, for a
art, fully legalized cannabis.'

Jilliam Burroughs *(right)*

urroughs enjoyed any and all drugs, including
ashish and grass. He moved to eastern Texas
ith his wife, Joan Vollmer Adams, where they
ew a cash crop of marijuana. After Burroughs
ccidentally shot Joan dead, he fled to Tangiers,
orocco, and partook of various cannabis
roducts, including kif pipes with sinsemilla,
ajoun sweets and strong hashish. He wrote the
assic *Naked Lunch* while high on reefer and
annabis confectionery.

In 1956 Burroughs wrote an article for the
ritish Journal of Addiction where he listed every
ug he'd tried. On using cannabis while
ithdrawing from heroin, he stated, 'In late or
ght withdrawal [cannabis] relieves depression
d increases the appetite, in acute withdrawal
unmitigated disaster. (I once smoked
arijuana during early withdrawal with
ghtmarish results.) Cannabis is a sensitizer. If
u feel bad already it will make you feel worse.'
urroughs died in 1997, aged 83.

ack Kerouac

erouac helped kick off the Beat Generation with
e ground-breaking novel, *On The Road*. In
J39 he graduated from high school and started

hanging out at the Harlem jazz clubs. It was there
that he smoked marijuana for the first time and
soon became a life-long convert. *On The Road*,
like Burrough's *Naked Lunch*, was created in a
stream of consciousness while constantly stoned

113

"In the early moments of getting stoned you are seized by an outrageous hilarity, irresistible and ludicrous.... The most simple words and trivial ideas assume bizarre and fantastic shapes; you feel astonished not to have realized their simplicity before" *Charles Baudelaire*

"Is marijuana addictive? Yes, in the sense that most of the really pleasant things in life are worth endlessly repeating"

Richard Neville, **Playpower**

and told of Kerouac's adventures of travelling across the USA. His work often referred to reefer: 'Victor proceeded to roll the biggest bomber anybody ever saw. He rolled (using brown bag paper) what amounted to a tremendous Corona cigar of tea. It was huge. Dean stared at it, popeyed. Victor lit it and casually passed it around. To drag on this thing was like leaning over a chimney and inhaling. It blew into your throat in one great blast of heat. We held our breaths and all let out simultaneously. Instantly, we were all high.' In 1969 he tragically fell victim to booze and drank himself into eternal oblivion aged 47.

Above: The troubled genius Jack Kerouac, one of the original beat writers and puffers.

Norman Mailer *(right)*

The novelist, now aged 81, achieved fame in 1948 with *The Naked and the Dead*, which was based on his experiences during World War II. After the war, Mailer worked as a scriptwriter in Hollywood, as much of his work was refused by publishers. But in the mid-1950s he became famous as an anti-establishment essayist. Mailer was smoking prodigious quantities of grass during that decade. 'He was on pot a lot. He

didn't smoke it like other people would drink beer at parties, you know, to get mellow. He treated it as a nearly religious experience,' said Mary V. Dearborn, Mailer's biographer. 'He thought of smoking a joint the way others would think of taking an LSD trip. And I think he got higher than other people do on pot.' Things went bad in 1960 when Mailer stabbed his wife Adele. 'I think the combination of marijuana and heavy alcohol use... it was hard for him to connect with reality,' said Dearborn. 'He got deeper and deeper into self-referential thinking. The amount of drugs he was doing, and the tailspin it sent him into... he wasn't a casual user. He was fucking with his own head...' Mailer himself confirmed, 'One's condition on marijuana is always existential.' Unsurprisingly, he's been married six times and has nine children. He has won two Pulitzer Prizes, for *Armies of the Night* (1968) and *The Executioner's Song* (1979).

Oscar Wilde

The Victorian wit and playwright was not only partial to buggery, but also blow. In January 1895 on a trip to Algiers with 'Bosie' (Lord Alfred Douglas) – his homosexual lover – they both used it, as Wilde wrote: 'It is quite exquisite: three puffs of smoke and then peace and love.' He also enjoyed opium cigarettes. Wilde's friend in Paris, Marcel Schwob, wrote in 1891: '[Wilde] never stopped smoking opium-tainted Egyptian cigarettes. A terrible absinthe-drinker, through which he got his visions and desires.' No wonder Wilde was popular with the flower children of the Sixties.

Alexander Dumas

In Paris the infamous Le Club de Hachichins was the place to be seen for all aspiring writers, artists and stoners in the mid-19th century. It was set up by Theophile Gautier, and its members included literati such as Victor Hugo and Honore de Balzac, and artist Eugene Delacroix. They gathered at Paris' Gothic Pimodan House (Hotel Lazun) to partake of syrupy hashish mixed with strong Arabic coffee and blow their brilliant minds. Dumas, author of the classics *The Three Musketeers* and *The Count of Monte Cristo*, was initially banned by members of the club, as they considered him bourgeois – his associations with counts and countesses and friendship with King Louis Philippe made him uncool to the 19th-century beatniks. But eventually he blagged his way in. Dumas never wrote about his own visionary experiences under the drug, but *The Count of Monte Cristo* includes an encounter with a hashish-ingesting sailor, revealing that Dumas knew how to bogart a joint or two.

Allen Ginsberg

Ginsberg was the poet of the Beat generation. Alongside Kerouac and Burroughs, he was a huge smoker. He became almost evangelical in his zeal to get pot decriminalized. He wrote a spliff-driven rant/essay, 'The Great Marijuana Hoax', about his attitude to the use of cannabis.

Above: Allen Ginsberg (with sign) and friends try to raise American consciousness while freezing their asses off.

He believed it isn't a drug, offering an easy escape, but rather a natural agent (a herb) that offers the chance to experience a true expansion of consciousness, an increase in awareness, a general improvement and heightening of perception of all kinds, particularly as 'a useful catalyst for specific optical and aural aesthetic perceptions'. Ginsberg stated he had spent about

Charles Baudelaire *(left)*

Baudelaire joined Le Club de Hachichins in Paris after being introduced to its founder Theophile Gautier by painter Fernand Boissard. Baudelaire wrote how after consuming cannabis, 'on occasion the personality disappears. That concentration on the external, which is the hallmark of all great poets and master comedians grows and dominates your outlook'. Baudelaire rarely tripped out himself, preferring to watch his mates make tits of themselves. He eventually wrote *Les Paradis Atificiels* (Artificial Paradises), chronicling his experimentation with hashish and opium. But Baudelaire was hamstrung by Catholic guilt and suffered great despair. He considered himself a failure, was an alcoholic and an opium addict, and died of syphilis he'd contracted in his youth. Bummer.

Hunter S. Thompson *(right)*

The godfather of Gonzo glorified grass like no other: 'I have always loved marijuana. It has been a source of joy and comfort to me for many years. And I still think of it as a basic staple of life, along with beer and ice and grapefruits – and millions of Americans agree with me.' Thompson made a name for himself as a sports writer for the fledgling *Rolling Stone*, but soon turned his assignments on himself reporting about his massive drug-fuelled binges and bizarre encounters, and founding gonzo writing, where the writer is more important than the story. His *Fear and Loathing in Las Vegas* is a classic of the

as much time 'high as I have spent in movie theatres – sometimes three hours a week, sometimes twelve or twenty or more, with about the same degree of alteration of my normal awareness.' His awareness and campaigning ended when he died in 1997.

genre, detailing Thompson digesting just about every drug known to man: 'We had two bags of grass, seventy-five pellets of mescaline, five sheets of high-powered blotter acid, a saltshaker half-full of cocaine, and a whole galaxy of uppers, downers, laughers, screamers.... Also, a

quart of tequila, a quart of rum, a case of beer, a pint of raw ether, and two dozen amyls. Not that we needed all that for the trip, but once you get into a serious drug collection, the tendency is to push it as far as you can.'

Hashish Hollywood

Charlize Theron *(left)*

The Oscar-winning actress was caught in 2002 by the *National Enquirer*, taking a long blast from a bong at a pool party at her house in LA. This wasn't any old bong, but a cool home-made affair made from an apple, indicating that the South African-born star knows some true stoner experts. A guest said, 'She sucked the smoke from a hole on the side of the apple, coughed a bit, started giggling hysterically and then passed the apple bong to her friends. Hippies in the Sixties used to smoke pot out of apples all the time, and my guess was that Charlize's Granny Smith was filled with something other than tobacco, since she was already smoking a cigarette.'

Jay and Silent Bob

The true stoner stars of every Kevin Smith film to date (*Clerks*, *Mallrats*, *Chasing Amy*, and *Dogma*) finally achieved top billing in 2001's *Jay and Silent Bob Strike Back*. The modern day Cheech and Chong head to Hollywood when a film is about to be made based on their

Above: New Jersey slackers, Jay and Silent Bob, skin up in *Chasing Amy*.

comicbook superhero alter egos, Bluntman and Chronic. Jay and Bob (played by Jason Mewes and Smith) are all about, as Jay so eloquently raps, 'Smokin' weed, smokin' wizz, doing coke, drinkin' beers, drinkin' beers, beers, beers, rollin' fatties, smokin' blunts. Who smokes the blunts? We smoke the blunts!'

Tommy Chong

The second half of the legendary cannabis comedy duo Cheech and Chong, Tommy fell out with Cheech Marin after the latter gave up the weed and became a Hollywood shill doing voice-overs for Disney films. But Chong, 65, kept the faith, and it cost him when he was sentenced on 11 September 2003 to nine months in prison for conspiring to sell bongs and other drug paraphernalia over the Internet. The conviction was part of the US Department of Justice's sting,

Above: The original Hollywood hempers, Cheech Marin and Tommy Chong, guest star on *Gardener's World Question Time*. Cheech is sporting a NORML T-Shirt.

Operation Pipe Dreams. Despite their falling out, Cheech supported his ex-partner in the *LA Times*: 'These are the same kinds of simpletons we were fighting when we made *Up in Smoke* [1978], in terms of a repressive administration. That Tommy Chong is going to prison for this is a total miscarriage of justice. The administration should hang its head in shame.'

Larry Hagman

Old JR of Dallas fame described in his 2002 autobiography, *Hello Darlin'*, the first time he tried pot. 'I was down in Acapulco, and Jack [Nicholson] said, "You're drinking too much," and he was right. So he said, "Smoke this stuff," and I did, and it opened me up to a lot of things too. It's a calming drug. It's not a drug; it's an herb.' Although Hagman says he no longer tokes, he explained that marijuana 'is benign compared to alcohol. When you come right down to it, alcohol destroys your body and makes you do violent things. With grass you sit back and enjoy life.'

Morgan Freeman

In April 2003 actor Freeman told *The Guardian* newspaper that he'd stopped using cocaine and other 'hard drugs', but that he would 'never give up on the ganja'.

Freeman, 65 – who has been nominated for three Academy Awards –- called marijuana, in true Rastafarian style, 'God's own weed' and explained how Moses' encounter with the 'burning bush' was an early Biblical reference to the spiritual benefits of cannabis use.

Freeman made his Broadway debut in the musical *Hello, Dolly!* with fellow stoner Cab Calloway, and went on to play everyone from a chauffeur (*Driving Miss Daisy*) through the President of America (*Deep Impact*) to God Himself (*Bruce Almighty*).

Shaggy and Scooby-Doo

Both the cartoons and the 2002 film are rife with pot references, including Shaggy's love interest, called Mary Jane. Shaggy and Scooby have long been tagged as a pair of puffers thanks to their heavy appetites, predilection to seeing ghosts and devotion to the energy-enhancing 'Scooby Snacks' – all of which reveal their stoner status. Scooby Doobie Doo's middle name being a synonym for a joint provides the final confirmation. 'Scooby Snack' has even become a generic term for party drugs like Ecstasy and magic mushrooms.

The stoned Scooby-Doo has also inspired songs by bands including Fun Lovin' Criminals and Cypress Hill. In 1998 billionaire media mogul Ted Turner was approached by Cable Sitters, a media-monitoring group who complained that Scooby-Doo is 'laced with subliminal drug references' and demanded that Turner's Cartoon Network stop broadcasting re-runs of the series. Tokin' Turner wisely ignored them.

Robert Mitchum

The ex-boxer, escaped con and tough guy film actor, who once said, 'I don't care what I play; I'll play Polish gays, women, midgets, anything,' was the first celebrity victim of marijuana prohibition. He was arrested in blonde starlet Lila Leeds' house in Laurel Canyon, California, after a 1948 stakeout. Mitchum told his lawyer: 'Well, this is the bitter end of everything – my career, my marriage, everything.' When questioned about his drug of choice he replied, 'The only effect that I ever noticed from smoking marijuana was a sort of mild sedative, a release of tension when I was overworking. It never made me boisterous or quarrelsome. If anything, it calmed me and reduced my activity.' He was sentenced to 60 days on an honour farm/open prison, but emerged robust as ever, saying, 'It's just like Palm Springs without the riffraff,' and, 'The only difference between me and my fellow actors is that I've spent more time in jail.' Mitchum died in 1999 aged 79.

Jack Nicholson

'My point of view, while extremely cogent, is unpopular… that the repressive nature of the legalities vis-à-vis drugs are destroying the legal system and corrupting the police system.' So said the dope-smoking star of numerous films, including the seminal stoner classic *Easy Rider*. Not only has Jack been actively outspoken in his support of cannabis, but he's turned fellow actors on to it, such as Larry Hagman.

Robert Altman

The director of *M*A*S*H*, *Short Cuts* and *The Player* was a heavy drinker, 'but the alcohol affected my heart rather than my liver. So I stopped. I smoke grass now. I say that to everybody, because marijuana should be

Above: Hollywood heartthrob Robert Mitchum emerges from two months in the slammer for possession of the wacky baccy in 1948.

legalized. It's ridiculous that it isn't. If at the end of the day I feel like smoking a joint I do it. It changes the perception of what I've been through all day.' Like Willie Nelson, Altman is also on the advisory board of NORML.

Jane and Peter Fonda

The Fonda siblings are possibly the loudest and longest proponents of hashish in Hollywood. Both have toked on-screen and off, and Jane was once married to counterculture radical Tom Hayden. In 1980 Jane appeared in *9 to 5*, toking up with her fellow secretaries, yet she was a known puffer some years before that. In 1967 she appeared on the cover of *Red Dirt Marijuana*, an anthology of short stories by Terry Southern, who helped write *Easy Rider*, and in 1970, *Uncensored Tabloid Magazine* called Jane 'Hollywood's wildest pot-smoking rebel.'

Easy Rider, released in 1969, saw Jane's brother, Peter, finance his cross-country motorcycle trip with a coke deal, trip on acid, and introduce Jack Nicholson's character to marijuana. Jane maintains her publicly pot-head ways. An article in the June 2001 *Daily Variety* had film reviewer Rex Reed outing both Fonda and himself. The article explained how Reed had profiled Jane Fonda as she sat smoking marijuana. 'Her comment when the piece came out,' said Reed, 'was, "I don't mind that he said I was smoking pot. I only minded that he didn't say he was smoking it, too."'

Cary Grant and Dyan Cannon

To the suave film actor, smoking a bud would have been like having a cup of tea – in the late Fifties, Grant went through over 100 LSD therapeutic trips. He was married to *Ally McBeal*'s Dyan Cannon, who was a serious smoker from 1962 to 1968: 'I was addicted to marijuana,' claimed the actress. 'I would have to have a puff off a joint before every take. I'd run out to the bathroom and come back...' Cannon eventually considered herself a 'marijuana addict', which led to her quitting pot and finding Jesus. 'I was going to go make a film in Greece, and if they caught you with this much marijuana, they threw you in jail, no questions asked. I was trying to stuff it in my deodorant bottles.... And I thought, what I am doing? Is this thing bigger than me?'

Rogue Scientists, Free Thinkers and Outsiders

Carl Sagan

Under the pseudonym Mr X, Sagan wrote his classic pot-smoking essay in the 1971 book *Reconsidering Marijuana*. In it, he said marijuana inspired some of his intellectual work. 'I can remember one occasion, taking a shower with my wife while high, in which I had an idea on the origins and invalidities of racism in terms of Gaussian distribution curves,' wrote the author of the popular science books *Cosmos* and *Contact*. 'I wrote the curves in soap on the shower wall, and went to write the idea down.' Far out. Sagan later wrote, 'I find that today a single joint is enough to get me high… in one movie theatre recently I found I could get high just by inhaling the cannabis smoke which permeated the theatre.' Sagan's former wife, Ann Druyan, is a director of NORML. Sagan died of pneumonia in 1996 aged 62.

Timothy Leary *(right)*

The LSD guru is more renowned for his connections to acid than pot, but it was marijuana that brought him his biggest trouble. In 1965 he was busted for possession of cannabis on the way back from Mexico. He was sent down for an excessive 10 years, but was busted out by the revolutionary group the Weathermen and split to Afghanistan. He set himself up as a hashish smuggler and became a precursor to that other super-smuggler, Howard Marks. Leary was busted by the DEA in Kabul in 1974 and served another three years in a US jail before being released after grassing his mates up to the FBI. He died in 1996.

Aleister Crowley

'The wickedest man in the world', whose maxim 'Do what thou wilt' led him to doing just about every conceivable drug on the planet, including the chronic. 'The Great Beast' was a British occultist, mystic, poet, mountain climber, sexual revolutionary and social critic. He studied mysticism in every guise, formed his own religion (Thelema) and was a member of the 'magick' group, the Hermetic Order of the Golden Dawn. He wrote numerous books – both fiction and essays – including *Diary of a Drug Fiend* and *Psychology of Hashish: An Essay on Mysticism*. Crowley died a heroin addict, alone in a boarding house in Hastings, England, in 1947.

Richard Feynman

The renegade physicist, Nobel Laureate (1965), best-selling author and member of the Presidential Commission that investigated the Challenger disaster experimented with pot and floatation tanks early in life. He was a popular lecturer who was widely known for his insatiable curiosity, gentle wit, brilliant mind and playful temperament. His 1985 book, *Surely You're Joking, Mr Feynman*, was on the *New York Times* best-seller list for 14 weeks. Bizarrely, for a dope-lovin' peacenik, he was also a member of the team that developed the first atomic bomb at Los Alamos. Feynman died in 1988 from stomach cancer. His last words were, 'I'd hate to die twice. It's so boring.'

Howard Marks *(right)*

'Mr Nice' was one of the most prolific marijuana smugglers in the Seventies and Eighties. The modest Welshman dealt with every shady organization from the CIA to the IRA. At his peak in the mid-1980s Marks had 43 aliases and 89 phone lines, and owned 25 companies throughout the world, including bars, recording studios and offshore banks – all money-laundering covers for his dope dealing. At the height of his career the Oxford graduate was smuggling consignments of up to 30 tons from Pakistan and Thailand to America and Canada. Many years later Marks was finally busted, like Timothy Leary before him, by a world-wide DEA operation. Sentenced to 25 years in prison at

Terre Haute Penitentiary, Indiana, he was released after seven in April 1995. He then wrote his memoirs, which became a best-seller and made him a media celeb, writing articles for magazines, appearing on television and furthering the argument for legalization of cannabis. He is the most vocal and prominent toker in the UK, even running for Parliament on the pro-cannabis manifesto.

Friedrich Nietzsche

The German philosopher was a brilliant student and became Professor of Classical Philosophy at the University of Basel in 1869. He retired in 1879 due to poor health (possibly syphilis), which would plague him for the rest of his life. Like Queen Victoria, he was prescribed cannabis tincture as a possible cure-all. But Nietzsche still knew how to party: 'Believe me! The secret of reaping the greatest fruitfulness and the greatest enjoyment from life is to live dangerously!' From 1880 he led a wandering, gypsy-like existence, writing most of his major works during this period. He finally collapsed in Italy in 1889, wearing only underwear and tearfully embracing a horse because it had been beaten. He never recovered, and spent the last 10 years of his life insane and unaware of the success of his work.

His most well-known work, *Thus Spake Zarathustra* (1885) chronicled the wanderings and teachings of a philosopher, self-named Zarathustra after the founder of Zoroastrianism. Coincidentally, the original Persian prophet Zoroaster, in 550BC, gave hemp first place in the sacred text, the *Zend-Avesta*, which listed over 10,000 medicinal plants. Later, *Thus Spake Zarathustra* was misappropriated by the Nazis to further their cause.

Gilbert Shelton

The comicbook guru of ganja, Shelton is the creator of the most instantly recognizable icons of pot culture, the Fabulous Furry Freak Brothers.

Shelton created the trippin' trio (Phineas Freak, Fat Freddy and Freewheelin' Franklin) back in 1968 and they took off immediately, becoming the doyens of the counterculture. Their wild misadventures while eternally pursuing quality grass, and Fat Freddy's unnamed cat made them a global success, and despite there only ever being 13 comics, the series has been in constant print for over 35 years. Shelton has always worn his inspiration on his sleeve: 'I've always smoked just as much as I could get away with.' He also coined the phrase, 'Dope will get you through times of no money better than money will get you through times of no dope,' a maxim taken up by millions of stoners around the world. Texan-born Shelton now lives in Paris, France.

Shiva *(left)*

According to mythology, the Hindu god was not only responsible for the creation of the first marijuana plant but also its use. One day Shiva saw fellow God, Krishna, bathing in the Ganges and become so enraged with jealously at the blue-skinned one's beauty that Shiva fired an arrow at him. The wounded Krishna staggered to the shore, and where a drop of his divine blood fell grew the first ganja plant. Shiva later rested by the plant, began to chew the leaves and, won over by its euphoric effects, adopted it as his talisman. Today, followers of Shiva, Shaivaites and holy Sadhus, smoke enormous amounts of ganja in chillums as sacrament and in praise of the doped-out demi-god.

Sheikh Hasan ibn al-Sabah

Hasan grew to power by forming the cult of Ismaili hitmen, the Assassins. The name came from hashishin or hashish-eater. From his Eagle's Nest fortress in the Persian mountains the 'Old Man of the Mountains' converted his fanatical followers by not promising paradise, fulfilment and eternal joy to people. He actually showed them it, in the form of an artificial paradise, where fountains gushed sweet-scented waters and every sensual wish was granted. Hasan attracted young men, aged 12–20: especially those he marked out as potential killers. He drugged them and placed them in a garden. 'Upon awakening from this state of lethargy, their senses were struck by all the delightful objects, and each perceiving himself surrounded by lovely damsels… serving him with delicious viands and exquisite wines, until… he believed himself assuredly in Paradise, and felt an unwillingness to relinquish its delights.' After four or five days they pledged allegiance to Hasan, believing that only he could give the Key to Paradise.

Another trick of Hasan's was to dig a deep pit in the floor of his audience chamber. One of his disciples stood in it so only his head and neck were visible. Around the neck was placed a circular dish, giving the impression there was a severed head on a metal plate on the floor with some fresh blood poured around the head for effect. Recruits were brought in. 'Tell them,' commanded the chief, 'what thou hast seen.' The 'severed head' then described the delights of Paradise. 'You have seen the head of a man who died, whom you all knew. I have reanimated him to speak with his own tongue.' Later, the disciple's head was treacherously severed for real and placed where the faithful would see it. The effect of this gruesome conjuring trick increased the enthusiasm for martyrdom, as did copious amounts of hash munching. Today, the sect still exists in the form of the Ismailis, whose undisputed chief, endowed by them with divine attributes, is the Aga Khan.

Busted!

It doesn't matter whether you are a major sensimilla smuggler or a first-time smoker with a single joint, 'The Man' will come down on you just as hard. Unbelievably, over 12 million citizens have been arrested on marijuana charges in the US since 1965. A marijuana arrest now occurs every 45 seconds in the Americas, and even celebrities aren't safe from the prying eyes of an outmoded law.

In fact, the US government, the DEA and its predecessor, the Federal Bureau of Narcotics have championed the arrests of famous citizens as a show of force and resolve, and as a supposed deterrent since the 1930s. Infamous busts of stars have included director Oliver Stone in 1999, James Brown, the Godfather of Soul, in 1998, and David Bowie and Iggy Pop in 1976. But two of the most high-profile, and numerous, busts, belong to just two bands, the Rolling Stones and the Beatles.

Mick Jagger and Keith Richard were arrested a the latter's home in East Sussex in 1967 (see World's Top 50 Potheads). The whole farce ultimately went in favour of the Stones, with politicians and newspapers supporting them. But Jagger's problems didn't end there. Two years later, after a tip-off from 'an informant', the police raided Jagger's and then-current girlfriend Marianne Faithfull's Chelsea home in May 1969. Officers went into the house and claimed to find some cannabis in a white Cartier box on a table

Above: 'You're fuckin' nicked, me old beauty!' Mick Jagger at one of his numerous court appearances.

nd a large lump of hashish in a drawer. 'I had o knowledge there was any cannabis in the ouse,' claimed Mick. After formal charges, and n the way home from the police station, Jagger aid to Faithfull. 'You saw that big piece of hash, idn't you? Are you sure it wasn't yours?' She

confirmed it wasn't. 'We've been planted, haven we?' said Mick. Jagger appointed Michael Havers, who'd been his lawyer back in 1967, bu was still fined £200 for possessing cannabis and made to pay 50 guineas [£52.50] costs. But the Stones are having the last laugh. They are producing a new film about the 1967 bust, with actor Nigel Havers playing his lawyer father.

The Rolling Stones' main musical competition the Beatles, were 'switched on' to weed by Bob

Dylan in 1964. The Fab Four then got into lots of trouble with the law. In 1968 John Lennon was sub-letting a maisonette in Marylebone, London, from fellow Beatles member, Ringo Starr. Lennon was living there with his new girlfriend Yoko Ono, and it was here that police raided at 11:30 a.m. on 18 October. They discovered a small quantity of cannabis resin, 27.3g (1oz), in an envelope in a suitcase, and a sniffer dog discovered a further 191.8g (7oz) in a binocular case on the living room mantelpiece. This was enough to secure John and Yoko's arrest. Lennon initially claimed that the drugs were planted by the police, but subsequently pleaded guilty to the charges on 1 November. His conviction on 28 November saw him fined £150 plus costs.

The raid had repercussions for many involved. Between the raid and conviction, Yoko suffered a miscarriage at Queen Charlotte's Hospital, London, on 21 November. As a result of Lennon's arrest, Ringo Starr's landlords Brymon Estates won an injunction against Ringo to prevent 'illegal, immoral or improper' use of the maisonette, after which Starr sold his lease. Presumably he couldn't guarantee those conditions.

Lennon's bust would continue to haunt him for years to come. Six months after his conviction, the US Embassy in London refused to issue Lennon a visa because of his arrest. So on 24 May 1969, John and Yoko flew to the Bahamas instead. When he was eventually allowed into the US, Lennon applied for permanent residency. However, he inadvertently made an enemy of the dope-despising President, Richard Nixon, by openly praising pot and condemning the Vietnam War. Lennon gave his first US gig in five years on 10 December 1971 as part of a benefit gig for jailed activist John Sinclair, who was busted for possession of two joints. Nixon set the FBI to spy on Lennon and came very close to deporting him, using his cannabis conviction as an excuse.

In 1969, a year after Lennon's original bust, another Beatle, George Harrison, was also arrested after they raided his home in London and found 570 grains (36 grams) of pot.

Paul McCartney was arrested five times, all after the Beatles had split. On 10 August 1972 he and his wife Linda were nicked in Sweden after postal officials intercepted a parcel of hashish addressed to their band, Wings. Eight years later McCartney was busted again, this time at Narita International Airport, Japan, for possession of 215g (7.5oz) of marijuana. He spent nine days in jail before being deported on 25 January 1980.

In a 2002 Time/CNN poll, 72 per cent of Americans felt that people arrested with small amounts of marijuana should not do any jail time, while 34 per cent are now in favour of complete legalization, compared with 18 per cent in 1986. It appears that the public's attitudes are mellowing, even if the law enforcement agencies' aren't.

Left: Old Bill overkill. John Lennon and the obviously distressed Yoko Ono are arrested in 1968.

Chapter 5

Around the World in 80 Tokes

Ever since the Sixties, stoners have been travelling the globe looking for the best gear. But which countries produce the best hash and grass? More importantly, wha are the risks and rewards in cannabis tourism?

Around the World in 80 Tokes

The semi-mythical 'Hippie Trail' that developed in the Sixties was seen as a rite of passage for many young adventurers. Born out of cheaper mass travel by plane and the urge to discover one's spiritual self, a whole generation took off around the planet on a journey that broadened the mind in more ways than one.

The trail, in its shortest version, went to Morocco via the Mediterranean island of Ibiza. However, more adventurous travellers went as far afield as Turkey, Iraq, Iran, Afghanistan, Nepal, India and, ultimately, Thailand and Vietnam. The one thing all these countries had in common was they all produced large crops of marijuana, a very important motivation in the golden era of 20th-century pot-smoking. These days, when international travel is like getting on a bus, it's hard to imagine how difficult and daunting the trail really was. But the allure of experiencing foreign culture, possible spiritual enlightenment, romance of the road and cheap drugs was strong.

As one US traveller recalled, 'Fuelled by ganja and hashish picked up along the way, American, European and Australian hippies met, mingled, exchanged body fluids and explored whatever highs and lows that travel presented.'

Even today, students in their 'gap year' between school and university make the same

Above: These days it's no longer necessary to globetrot for grass, as quality weed invariably finds its way to the West's high-streets from Baltimore to Brixton.

pilgrimages their parents made decades earlier. Oz band Men at Work exulted the quest in their 1982 hit 'Down Under': 'Travelling in a fired-out combie/On a hippie trail, head full of zombie' – a 'combie' being a VW camper van, and 'zombie' a potent strain of grass. While in these uncertain times – thanks to the never-ending 'War on Terrorism' – some of the traditional hippie hangouts are now more dangerous or near-suicidal, others still welcome tokin' travellers with open arms and a lit joint.

War on Drugs

From the kids of Grange Hill and Nancy Reagan just saying 'no' to the millions of dollars poured into high profile raids and drug programs in America, the War On Drugs is big business... but is anyone winning?

In January 2004, the Labour government took what some see as a progressive step towards accepting the use of cannabis in the UK. The drug was re-classified from class B to class C, dramatically reducing the prison sentences and fines that can be given to users or suppliers. However, far from being a victory to the 'enemy' in the War On Drugs it will just lead to more casualties through confusion among users and, worst of all, the UK's police, where the lack of a national policy has led to smokers being left to toke in peace in Brixton, but banged up in Scotland.

The roots of the War On Drugs can be traced back to '30s America, when marijuana was singled out as the cause of society's ills. Reams could be written on the real reasons behind marijuana's illegality. Much of it had a lot to do with the price of paper and how hemp was offering a cheaper alternative – a problem for well-connected media magnet William Randolph

Right: Spliff Wars: Attack of the Cannabis. Guerrilla gardeners planted seeds in flowerbeds outside Bath police station in the UK.

Hearst, who used his newspapers to run campaigns against hemp and his connections in the government to finally get it outlawed in 1937. Since then it has been lumped in with all illegal drugs and its users locked up, many for small counts of possession.

Surprisingly, America was just coming out of a period of prohibition, an attempt to control another powerful drug, alcohol, quite openly admitting its failure. Has it had any better luck

Above: Jazz drummer legend Gene Krupa was just one of the many famous casualties in the War on Drugs.

with marijuana? In 2002 the American police arrested 697,082 people for marijuana offences - 45% of all drug related arrests. Last year the US government spent $19 billion on its war against drugs, $600 a second and yet the problem still continues.

This isn't a winnable war; at best it is a good soundbite. What is needed is an adult debate, free from the emotional baggage drugs carry with them, but while political parties score points off each other over their differing drug policies, who is prepared to take this momentous step?

Whether cannabis, one of the least harmful drugs, legal or illegal, should even be included in this discussion or just legalized is another matter.

Below: Governments still fail to differentiate between heroin and the herb.

BOYCOTT WHITE POWDER BRING BACK HERB!

WE ARE COMING!

Morocco

Morocco is one of the largest producers of cannabis resin, the country's largest cash crop, worth about £1.4 billion (US$2.5 billion) every year. It is usually ranked above orange groves, date palms, tourism, fisheries and phosphate mining as one of the few capitalist success stories. The UN and CIA claim the country produces at least 13,500kg (30,000lb) of hashish annually, and satellite photos have revealed that roughly 220,000 acres are dedicated to hemp horticulture during the pot-growing season (March to early September). The mind-blowing scale of Morocco's cultivation can be seen in photos of huge clouds of male cannabis pollen that shroud Northern Africa and Southern Europe when the country's plants are in full bloom.

In the late Fifties and Sixties, the lure of marijuana and young men attracted the gay literati, from William Burroughs (see Top 50 Greatest Potheads) to Tennessee Williams and hippies by the busload. Although these two attractions are now illegal in Morocco, gay sex and marijuana are still available everywhere in the country, but discretion is the key word. Much more smoking is going on than meets the eye – at home with friends, or quietly on the balconies above cafes while sipping mint tea.

Left: Despite the hard, red soil marijuana is successfully cultivated in the hillsides in the Rif mountain ranges of Morocco.

Scoring in Morocco isn't hard, but subtlety and caution should be taken. Travellers shouldn't buy anything on their first night in the country. Everyone can tell who's just arrived, and novices are likely to get burned or, worse, busted. Like most places in the world, the anti-grass laws are harsh – particularly for tourists – although, according to locals, the penalties for homegrown illegal tobacco are far worse than for marijuana.

Generally marijuana comes in the form of resin made into slates or balls, but kif is also very popular. Kif, also known as Primero or Supreme, is a traditional concoction made for centuries in Morocco that consists of indigenous tobacco and finely chopped marijuana, very similar to India's charas.

The other form of cannabis is in majoun confections. Esther Freud's 1992 novel, *Hideous Kinky*, tells the story of a mother who goes to Morocco on the hippie trail with her two young daughters. While there they partake of majoun. 'We handed over our dirham and pointed and whispered, "Majoun," as we had seen it done. We were handed a twist of newspaper inside which was a small lump of hashish pounded into a sweet like fudge. We sat at the table and took turns scraping fragments off with our teeth. It seemed to me the most delicious taste in the world. Sand mixed with honey and fried in a vat of doughnuts. We passed it back and forth, giggling a conspiracy of joy and adventure.'

In 2002 it was possible to buy several lumps of gold-coloured hashish each about the size of golf

Above: From the mountains of Morocco to the cafes of Amsterdam, hashish reaches its final destination.

balls for about £26 (US$45). To Western eyes, the sheer quantity for a relative pittance can cause the unwary toker to lose the plot. When Canadian author of *Pot Planet*, Brian Preston, was assured by his guide of the quality of the hashish, the Moroccan failed to grasp the dangers of international smuggling: 'Half a kilo, Brian! Very easy to hide in a suitcase for the

flight home!' Top marijuana is variously described by locals as Double Zero, Sputnik or Bob Marley, but the majority of hash is generally high-quality. Double Zero is sticky, golden-green and sweet smelling, and it bubbles when heated. However, knowing the local names is not enough; it's important to know the difference between first, second and third shakes.

Shakedown

The first shake involves Moroccans stretching a nylon mesh tight over the mouth of a plastic basin. They then crumble on top several sheaves of dried grass and lay a sheet of heavy plastic on top, pulling the whole affair tight with a noose of heavy rubber. Then they beat the outside of the bucket gently for 30 seconds. This causes only the pollen to fall through the mesh. What looks like an empty bucket to the beginner is now actually covered in a thin layer of pollen which, scraped together into a few scant grams of gold dust, can be heated and pressed in the palm of your hand into pure Double Zero cannabis resin. The second shake repeats the process, with a bit more violence, releasing smashed leaves and more quantity. That's what mostly gets exported. Third shake is everything else, including the kitchen sink. This process was introduced to Morocco in the Sixties by visiting hippie herbal horticulturists, and has been brought up to date in Amsterdam with the invention of Ice-O-Later bags.

Pipe Down and Smoke Up

The older generation, mostly in the countryside, still use long-stemmed sebsi pipes to smoke kif. Sebsis are fragile and often made from the hollowed stalk of a marijuana plant, with a tiny

Above: Even in Belgium blokes will offer you Brussels' best blow.

bowl on the end, just big enough to hold a pea-sized lump of cannabis. There is an expert method for loading a sebsi, involving flicking small amounts of kif powder into the bowl with a forefinger and thumb, packing it down tightly,

147

lighting, inhaling twice and then turning the pipe sideways, so that a sharp blow propels the small burnt coal out of the pipe. These days young Moroccans spurn the traditional kif pipes in favour of rolling their own.

'That's why I am staying with this riff'

The vast majority of Morocco's marijuana crop is grown in the forbidding Rif Mountain region in the northeast of the country. The Rif is a spectacular geological feature, stripped bare of its natural vegetation by centuries of overpopulation and irrational land use, causing the raw undulations of stone, peaks and valleys to be starkly exposed.

The Rif's fiercely independent residents, known as Riffies (hence reefers), live mostly in isolation, managing terraced farms, scant water supplies and ganja fields. Riffies are descended from the fierce tribal Berber warriors and have their own form of indigenous music, Rif rock, Morocco's equivalent of reggae. The Rif's own music, languages and customs mean that outsiders are not always welcome. In the heart of the Rif lies Ketama, the deadly, seedy city notorious as the capital of the Moroccan hash trade. This is a no-go zone, even for government troops, and running gun battles between them and the grass growers are common, usually with the latter winning. Despite these difficulties, the Moroccan government assured the United Nations in 2001 that the country would eliminate all internal hashish production by 2008. Realistically,

marijuana cultivation is tolerated because much of the Rif is unable to support other industries that would generate the £1.5–2.5 billion (US$2.5–3.5 billion) per year and 25,000 jobs that cannabis harvesting creates. 'Kif is the only plant that can grow here,' said one local. 'If it wasn't for kif, many families would starve.'

Ibiza

The Balearic island was the perfect stop-off on the original hippie trail, a short ferry ride on the way to Marrakech, Morocco, and many decided to simply stay put. In the 1960s, hippies started guerrilla gardening by sowing cannabis seeds across the island. Today, this means little patches of wild marijuana are scattered all over Ibiza. This was the hippies' way of spreading the love around. One Spanish love activist took it literally by encouraging his crops to grow by masturbating and smearing the 'success' all over the leaves, truly communing with nature.

More than anywhere else on the modern hippie trail, the toker will find a welcome here. The police generally turn a blind eye to drugs, but have been known to impose jail sentences for some drug-related crimes, primarily smuggling and dealing Class A's such as ketamine. Otherwise, smoking is pretty much accepted.

In the early 1970s the legendary clubs Pacha and Amnesia were born. They were classy affairs, more champagne and silver coke spoons than reefer and 'shrooms. They began to attract the jet-set party people, such as pop stoners Freddie

Mercury and James Brown. The club culture soon took off, and today's young dancers choose Ecstasy and cocaine over their parent's drugs of choice. The 1990s were more profit-driven, with super-clubs Cream, Ministry of Sound and Manumission arriving for the summer season. Manumission started in 1994, after brothers Mike and Andy arrived on the island intending to start parties in Morocco. But, like their hippie predecessors, they decided on Ibiza, and each year things got bigger, better and madder, until the club and its promoters came to embody the very essence of Ibiza debauchery.

Jamaica

While not traditionally part of the original hippie trail, tokers have been flooding to Jamaica in recent years because quality marijuana is less expensive there than anywhere else in the world. However, Jamaica is not 'Holland in the Caribbean'. It is essential to plan well and find ethical allies to safely enjoy the balmy weather, reggae music, spicy foods, sandy beaches and plentiful ganja of Bob Marley's homeland.

One such ally is marijuana activist Brother Leeroy Campbell, who – almost uniquely – runs a resort promising his guests a high-quality ganja experience. Campbell is a National Democratic Movement candidate for Parliament and an outspoken critic of the Government:

Left: A hippie trailblazer enjoys a nice cup of 'herbal' tea, while forgetting to leave Ibiza.

Grassology

An aeon of cannabis culture has inevitably lead to a massive vocabulary describing the plant, its use and effects. It may have all started with the Latin names *Cannabis Sativa* and *Cannabis Indica* (the two most common strains of the plant), but since its first recorded usage over 5,000 years ago Cannabis has adopted more terminology than any other drug.

The plant itself has numerous names depending on where in the world it is grown. Popular Seventies grass, Thai Stick unsurprisingly came from Thailand, Afghani comes from Afghanistan and the infamous Kush comes from the Kush region in Northern Sudan. Knowing where your weed comes from is increasingly rare, but hash smokers generally have a better idea as Red Leb (from the Lebanon), Rocky (from Morocco), Manali from the Kulu Valley in India, or for lucky visitors to Nepal, the legendary Nepalese Temple

Ball, all wear their origins on their sleeves. The generic term hash or hashish dates back to 12th Century Persia and the assassins (Ashishin) of al-Hasan ibn-al-Sabbah, who ingested copious amounts of cannabis before embarking on raids and assassinations.

Right: : A primo (excellent quality) slate/brick (lump) of hash (cannabis resin) all ready for skinning up (rolling into a joint) and toking (smoking).

Above: A stoner (person who smokes cannabis) enjoys a few blasts (inhalations) of his major league doobie (large marijuana cigarette) and gets wasted (euphoric).

However, in recent years hydroponic strains, those cultivated for their strength in tightly controlled circumstances, have taken their names from everything from people, effects and, most famously, their smell – Skunk isn't called that for

nothing. Visitors to Europe's marijuana capital, Amsterdam, may find themselves smoking Jack Herer (a potent weed named after the hemp hero author), taking a hit of Mr Nice, named in honour of the UK's biggest marijuana advocate Howard Marks, or having a toke on Netherlands' royalty, Queen Beatrix. Equally you can get high on Purple or Silver Haze, White Widow (so called because of its dense covering of white THC crystals), the vision-inducing Northern Lights or the quick-flowering Early Girl. Taste even comes into the equation when naming strains such as Bubble Gum or Juicy Fruit, but sometimes obvious is best – well, that's what the growers of Big Bud obviously thought when they crossed a couple of strains and came up with one that blossomed into massive buds.

The generic names for cannabis also have interesting origins. Marijuana, possibly the most used name for cannabis, is a slang Mexican term that was used by the Americans to specifically condemn the plant, its zombiefying effects and Mexicans in general, when there was no love lost between the nations. The popular use of Sensimilla for good weed comes from another Mexican Spanish term, this time meaning without seeds.

Some names are biblical, the common Rastafarian word for cannabis, 'herb', comes directly from Psalms 104:14, 'He causeth the grass to grow for the cattle, and herb for the service of man.' Many religious tokers happily question the right for governments to make cannabis illegal, when God quite specifically said he gave us all the plants for our use. It sheds a whole new light on the story of the burning bush' – another name for the cannabis plant due to its appearance. The widely used term weed' makes reference to the invasive nature of cannabis, and its ability to grow anywhere.

Even when buying the drug, you can't escape the slang terms for the amount you want, many of which have come about as part of a secret language enabling stoners to talk freely without ripping off any listening narcs. In the US small amounts are often referred to by cost; a dime bag is 1/16th of an ounce, an Abe would be a $5 bag, due to Abraham Lincoln's appearance on the $5 bill. The UK's Cannabis is usually sold by weight and rhyming slang has always been a popular way to let some know how much you want. A Henry is 1/8th of an ounce – from Henry the VIII, a Farmer's Daughter will get you a quarter, and those after half an ounce will probably be asking their dealer to bring a Scarf along when they next meet. As many of these terms are specific not only to certain areas, but also between certain groups of friends, its worth finding out exactly what you are asking for – you don't want to order a brick of hash expecting an ounce only to get a kilo to plough through (or perhaps you do).

All this before you even get to roll your first… well, what do you roll? In the UK it would probably just be a spliff or a joint and you may well skin up instead of rolling it, referring to the papers or skins (or in rhyming slang Vera Lynn's or Vera's). In the US you'd roll a Doobie, or if you want to smoke with the big boys, scoop out the tobacco from a cigar, fill it with Chronic (a generic US term for ultra-strong weed) and make yourself a Philly Blunt – named after its hometown, Philadelphia. Never mind just smoking it, instead you could have a toke, a hit or a puff. Remember not to Bogart it (keep hold on to the joint, named after the actor, Humphrey), pass it round and get high, stoned, wasted, whacked, mashed, bolloxed or fucked.

And when do you smoke? In cannabis mythology the magic time to blaze up is 4:20pm. Many bizarre theories abounded about the origin of the number 420 (four twenty) from Hitler's birthday, to penal codes or police radio codes or even references to horror writer HP Lovecraft. None of them are true. According to ex-*High Times* editor, Steven Hager, the term originated at San Rafael High School, in 1971, among a group of about a dozen pot-smoking students called the Waldos. 420 was shorthand for the time of day the group would meet to toke. This number soon became integrated into stoner culture and appears subliminally in many films including *Fast Times at Ridgemount High* and in *Pulp Fiction*, where most, but not all, of the clocks in are set to 4:20.

With so many codes and nicknames for dope it's enough to make your head spin. Literally.

Spliffs 2

'The revolution will succeed when Jamaicans are allowed to grow, sell and market marijuana and hemp for any purpose they want to,' said Campbell. 'From tourism to nutrition, Jamaica is uniquely able to save its people by running an economy based on the ganja plant. This common sense proposal is opposed by the US Government, some police forces and the fundamentalist churches, but the people are for it.

'Jamaica is a great place to enjoy the healing herb,' enthused Campbell. 'There are almost always going to be many opportunities for guests to get great ganja and see ganja growing.' Not all owners and managers of Jamaica's tourist establishments so openly advertize their ability to provide ganja, but many of them can discreetly get it or hook up a keen green fan with reputable dealers, but their paranoia is legitimate. Despite the recommendations of 2001's Chevannes Commission calling for decriminalization, ganja is still illegal.

Good vibes abound in Jamaica, but it pays not to be naïve: some people's friendliness is designed simply to open a tourist's wallet. When conducting ganja business, it pays to precisely spell out exactly what is required and make it clear – respectfully but firmly – that cons and bullying won't be tolerated. And, just as in any other travel situation, it's best to avoid places or circumstances that can lead to trouble. The island has pockets of poverty and crime that tourists should definitely stay away from. Both tourists and residents face regular highway checkpoints, shakedowns and

Above: A Jamaican farmer checks his jungle crop for that special Skunk smell.

ther police-generated dangers. Bribing one's way out of most ganja-related problems is the norm, but some tourists have suffered severe physical and financial discomfort because they were careless or unlucky to be possessing the holy herb at the wrong time or place.

Regardless of the risks, cannabis is widely available from private vendors, roadside shops and taxi drivers and masseuses. However, it's easy to get burned, as one joint-lovin' journalist found out in 2002, when he spent £400 (US$700) for 420g (15oz) of good-looking herb, only to be told he could have bought several kilos of cannabis for the same amount if he'd been a better negotiator. The average 'tourist price' for quality ganja back then was approximately £12–30 (US$20–50) per 28g (1oz).

About a third of the herb available is sativa and is generally seeded, but potent, fresh, tasty and organically grown. Varieties available include heirloom marijuana that had been smuggled into the Caribbean in the Sixties and Seventies, including classic Colombian Gold, Panama Red and Mexican Oaxacan, along with old Jamaican favourites like Collie Weed or Lamb's Bread.

Jamaican growers, hiding out from the police in the interior of the island, are plagued by bugs, droughts, robbers and non-equatorial cannabis genetics. Many sleep in their fields to guard them from thieves. Some ganja resorts and individuals offer tourists trips to see an 'authentic marijuana garden' for a fee. However, it is ill-advised to go into the bush without a security escort. And if

you're a narc, get your arse out of Jamaica, because the guys with machetes don't play games.

Afghanistan

During the 1960s and early 1970s, Afghani hash was considered the best in the world. Some ethnobotanists believe Afghanistan's earliest cannabis farmers mostly grew sativa varieties. But over time they switched to cultivating squat, tough, phat-leafed indica plants, which herbalists know as Hindu Kush, Afghani and the unimaginatively named Hashplant.

According to cannabis pioneer Wernard Bruining, Western hippies collected Afghan marijuana seeds and spread them across the world in the 1970s, particularly in Northern California, where the seeds became genetic ancestors for many of today's most popular strains. 'People who we call "the early Skunk pioneers" were experimenting with these Afghani seeds,' said Bruining, 'Afghan plants were highly sought after because they grew fast and short, were hardy, and produced huge tops full of resin. Some of them had the characteristic skunky smell and powerful body high that now identifies varieties known as Skunk.'

Mohammed Zahir Shah, the pro-cannabis monarch, governed Afghanistan from 1933–73, when he was overthrown by a jealous relative. During his reign, the King offered armed protection and horticultural advice to marijuana growers, encouraging them to increase their yield with modern fertilization techniques.

Personal Highs:

Dope D'ohs!

Everyone has a funny stoned story to tell, but spare a thought for the unlucky ones whose mashed-up minds made for mishaps. The following stoners contributed to the Darwin Awards (www.darwinawards.com), which commemorate those whose stupidity improves our gene pool by removing themselves from it.

In 2000 a herbalist horticulturist in Indiana, USA, managed to raise a nice healthy marijuana plant in his back garden, when tragedy struck. He received a phone call from the authorities saying he was busted, but they wouldn't press charges if he brought the bush down to his local police station, roots and all. He chopped down his 2.4m (8ft) plant and carried it to the Sheriff's office, where surprised officers arrested him for the felony of cultivation. The phone call was a prank.

But the most stupid and tragic stoner came from the sunshine state of Florida. On 6 July 1999 a naked man was found dead on the back of Tillikum, a killer whale at Sea World in Orlando, a victim of drowning or hypothermia in the 12°C (55°F) water. The body had scrapes on it, signifying that the victim had been dragged along the bottom of the tank.

He was identified as a marijuana-smoking drifter named Daniel, who previously lived at a Hare Krishna temple in Miami. There he had a great love of nature, writing in his journal and feeding wild birds in the temple garden. But Daniel had difficulty adjusting to the religion's a.m. waking-up time, their dietary prohibitions and their abstinence from liquor, drugs, sex and gambling. He left abruptly in the spring, saying, 'I want to be free. I want to travel around.'

A few days later, our intrepid stoner sneaked into Sea World and loitered near the whale pools until 10 p.m. closing, evading security. He stripped to his bathing trunks, scaled a 1m (3ft) Plexiglas barrier and climbed into Tillikum's freezing enclosure to re-enact *Free Willy*. The following morning an employee spotted Daniel's naked body draped just below Tillikum's dorsal fin. The medical examiner said that Tillikum had apparently tried to remove Daniel's shorts with his razor-sharp teeth. Biologists believed he probably played with Daniel like a toy, without realizing that he was a fragile human being.

The nature lover left few clues about his state of mind when he decided to commune with a carnivore the size of a bus. A joint was found inside his pile of clothes, but no admission ticket to Sea World. Park workers announced that Daniel had communed with sea mammals two years previously, when he jumped into the manatee tank, which is filled with warmer water and safer creatures. Tillikum is the largest killer whale in captivity, at 7m (22ft) and 4983kg (11,000lb), and was considered dangerous as he was never trained for human contact.

So remember, when stoned don't answer the phone or swim with carnivorous mammals with the word 'killer' in their name.

"But Daniel had difficulty adjusting to the religion's 4 a.m. waking-up time, their dietary prohibitions and their abstinence from liquor, drugs, sex and gambling."

The King's top aides were even allegedly involved in overt hashish smuggling. DEA officials even believed that the sovereign's private jet was used to smuggle tons of hashish to Italy and other European countries. In their heydays the southern city of Kandahar and the north-central city of Mazar-i-Sharif were surrounded by huge fields of cannabis, peppered with huts and barns where resin powder was stored and processed.

Afghani hash was known for its sticky, resiny, unadulterated colour and texture, its sweet, tangy

Above and right: Hemp harvesting in the Bekaa Valley, Lebanon. Much of the marijuana growing here is a family business and everyone helps out.

taste and its narcotic, dream-inducing high. Before US anti-drug pressure changed Afghanistan's cannabis policies in 1974, super-potent connoisseur hashish was available at teahouses inside Afghanistan, and as exported sticks, half moons, slabs and bricks with a wide array of colours, tastes and highs. 'Afghanistan people like hashish,' one Afghan smuggler in Holland said. 'They have special rooms and pipes to smoke it. It's not all just to sell [abroad]. You can go to special markets and shops to buy it, especially near the border with Pakistan.'

Afghan farmers, as in Morocco, use primitive methods such as hand irrigation and fertilization techniques to produce resin glands for the industry. It's hard work, as most of the country is barren desert with poor nutrient soils, erratic water supplies and dry, hot summers combined with harsh winters. The industry took a massive nosedive when the oppressive Taliban came to power, and since 11 September 2001 it has been hard going with the US invasion and war. Yet the hardy hemp hangs on, giggling in the face of these adversities, and the US-supported Northern Alliance is now starting to export some hash to Dutch coffee shops for £2,800 (US$5,000) per kilo.

But today's Afghani hash is considered a mid-grade product, slightly inferior to traditional hashish from Morocco, Nepal, India and Europe. It is only about 40 per cent as potent as the newest types of hashish, such as Ice-O-Later, Nederhash and Bubblehash, that are made using modern technology that results in a far purer product than can be produced by farmers in desert countries like Afghanistan.

The smuggler in Holland believed that Afghani hash had lost its sterling reputation because it was now a mixture of resin powders from different types of plants, screened through relatively large-bore screens, held together with honey, animal fat or tree sap. 'It is still stronger and better than marijuana, gram for gram,' the man said. 'It has a little dust in it from the winds, but it is a flower of the desert. With this war, we might not be able to get any here for a long time.'

India

The Indian subcontinent, along with China, is generally regarded as the original home of the herb.

Cannabis is available in three different forms in India. The first, bhang, is made from the leaves and stems of uncultivated plants and blended into a pleasant-tasting liquid concoction. Bhang has a long illustrious history of usage (see *Kama Sutra* of Cannabis). Today, it is used by labourers in

India in the same way as beer is used in the West – to unwind and chill out after a hard day's work – fortunately without the aggressive, wife-beating side-effect of booze. High-caste Hindus are not permitted to use alcohol, but they are allowed bhang at religious and marriage ceremonies and family festivals.

The second is ganja, more potent than bhang, made from the tops of cultivated plants. But the most potent form of marijuana is charas, which is similar to hashish and is obtained by scraping the resin from the leaves of the cultivated plants and compacting it into hard blocks. It is often hand-rubbed with local tobacco, similar to kif. The lower Indian castes often have a few pulls on a chillum or ganja pipe to relieve fatigue, to obtain a sense of well-being, to stimulate appetite and to enable them to bear more cheerfully the strain and monotony of daily routines. All the above could teach Western politicians an important lesson if they'd listen; a stoned population is a happy population.

How Green is My Valley

Much of India's pot is grown in the Himalayan foothills in the north. The smell of cannabis permeates the thin mountain air of the Kullu Valley, where Manali and surrounding villages have for decades drawn foreign pleasure-seekers, some of whom choose never to return home. Hemp grows wild and has been used for generations by villagers to make ropes and in handicrafts. Westerners began flocking here in the 1960s, on that yellow brick road of liberation known as the Hippie Trail. Since then hemp has become a much more profitable industry for smoking than weaving. Manali cannabis can fetch 1,000,000 rupees (£14,000/US$25,000) a kilogram on international markets. 35,000 foreigners visit the Kullu Valley each year to sample, and smuggle, the world-famous dope. The local weed includes the Afghan hybrid, AK-47, and the Central Asian Kazakhi.

In the valleys of Kullu and Manali below Chanderkhani Pass is a little hub of a hundred houses. This small village, popularly known in the Kullu valley as 'the Republic of Malana', is home to 1,000 locals. It has an immaculate system of self-governance, with its own President and Prime Minister. They are a unique tribe with special customs who live in a world of self-created autonomy and claim Greek descent – Alexander the Great's troops are said to have camped there in the 4th century BC. Every February Malana celebrates the Harlala mask dance festival. Everyone takes a bath and a group of people wearing nothing but cannabis leaves and demon-like masks dance around the houses spreading cow dung, which provides insulation from the cold. The shit-hot village has a reputation as the Amsterdam of the East, and the local drug scene has developed its own rituals, including full moon parties (which can now be seen in nearly every drug resort in the world from Goa to Thailand) and serious smoking sessions.

Above: Welcome to the wonderful world of Woodstock '99 weed! A dealer shares his wares 30 years after his parents did the same.

However, the Indian police are starting to crack down on local producers after numerous disappearances of Western tourists. The Kullu Valley police have seized as much grass in two years as they did for the whole of the 1990s. In 2001, police confiscated some 160kg (353lb) of cannabis in the valley and arrested 111 people, including 33 foreigners. 2002 saw the amount seized rise to 385kg (849lb), with 162 people, including 42 foreigners, arrested, mostly involved with smuggling.

While Manali is synonymous with drugs for many tourists, the town is also a celebrated starting point for Himalayan treks.

"Good wine needs no bush, and perhaps products that people really want need no hard-sell or soft sell push.
Why not?
Look at pot."

Ogden Nash, Most Doctors Recommend or Yours for Fast Fast Fast Relief

"Heroin in its pharmaceutical preparation, diamorphine, is available on prescription for people in pain and it's very mildly prescribed. So the law does not say that, because a drug is classed as illegal it therefore should not be available on prescription."

Jack Straw

Spliffs 2

It has also been a favourite haunt for Indian leaders escaping muggy New Delhi, perhaps for a spot of mountainous marijuana monging?

Beach Bliss or Damned Dope?

Further south, on the west coast of India, the paradise lost resort of Goa has long been a stop-off for travellers since the Summer of Love. With its golden beaches and swaying palms, it was hard to leave such a place, and the local charas didn't make it easier. Drawn by the tranquillity, yoga, tantric practices and cannabis, hundreds of Western wastrels ambled their way to the beaches, beach-front bars and cheap hotels.

The Eighties saw ravers pick up where their parents left off, organizing full-moon parties, getting henna tattoos, dropping Ecstasy and coming down on charas. Cannabis, although illegal, is still incredibly easy to come by even today, as one hashish holidaymaker recalled: 'All the chai tea houses on Kudu beach reportedly sold liquid acid, charas and opium along with pancakes, muesli, lassis and thalis...'

But be warned: India's cannaboid pleasures are not the only thing that'll get you high. The penalties are astronomical as well. In 1998 a German tourist, Olaf Wuemling, was busted by the Goan police for possession of 200g (6oz) of cannabis. He was sentenced to 10 years imprisonment and a large fine. He served five years, and was only released in 2003 after he was granted clemency by the President of India.

But there's another serpent in paradise apart

Above: The perfect ingredients for a lost weekend in Amsterdam: beer, bud and bong

from the law. As our cannabis tourist observed, '... and what one couldn't buy illegally from these sources was probably available over the counter from the chemist in Gokarna – including "industrial"-strength speed and Diazepam by the bucketload.' It's this darker side of narcotics that now threatens Goa, as more travellers switch from relatively benign cannabis to harder, uglier drugs like heroin and the horse tranquillizer ketamine, which is available over the counter in pharmacists for as little as £1.50 (US$2.50) a gram. Recent deaths and unscrupulous pharmaceutical traffickers are casting a shadow on the beaches.

Many of the traffickers deal in triangular trade, heading to the Manali valley in the summer to stock up on mountain marijuana and then bringing it back to Goa to sell to backpackers. Their profits are used to pick up ketamine, which is then sold in the UK.

But the local police deny there's a problem. Seva Dass, Goa's police chief, believed there was 'no heroin' in Goa. 'There is a problem with some drugs, mainly cannabis, but not with heroin,' he said. Locals say the government is playing down the problem to protect the tourist trade – 2,000,000 holidaymakers visited the state in 2002, including 100,000 Britons.

Locals look back on Goa's 'freak' days with nostalgia: 'There was pot and some LSD, and the glazed-eyed foreigners intrigued us,' said Anselmo Dias, who runs the Starway Shack in Baga, a fishing village. 'Now we are deep in the world of drug abuse.' So tokin' tourists should simply remember the words of Steppenwolf's song, 'The Pusher': 'You know, I've smoked a lot of grass/Oh Lord, I've popped a lot of pills/But I never touched nothing/That my spirit could kill…'

Thailand

Opium, heroin and marijuana are widely available in Thailand, but it is illegal to buy, sell or possess them in any quantity – unless you're a member of a northern province hill tribe, in which case opium for personal use is cool. But the illicit drug of choice among locals is MDA and the highly psychotic Ya Baa, smuggled in from Myanmar (Burma).

However, grass dominates the islands as hundreds of Westerners gather on beaches to get stoned and dance the night away at full moon parties. Undoubtedly there are hundreds of hidden plantations scattered around the endless list of islands in the south. In Alex Garland's cult novel, *The Beach*, the hero thinks he's hit the jackpot when he and his friends come across a sea of green: 'Etienne grinned. "Have you ever seen so much?" "Never…" I pulled a few leaves from the nearest bush and rubbed them in my hands. Etienne waded further into the plateau. "We should pick some, Richard," he said. "We can dry it in the sun and…" Then he stopped… I could literally see colour draining from his face. "This is a field," he said. I froze. "A field?" …We stared at each other. "Jesus Christ," I said slowly. "Then we're in deep shit."'

But as dangerous as Thai dope growers are, the government are no teddy bears either. To say that penalties for drug offences are stiff in Thailand is an understatement. They make Turkish prisons look like a holiday camp. Although tourists may only get a one-year prison sentence for possession of marijuana – still not any kind of fun – the deal for Thais is a whole lot worse. In 2003, Thailand's Prime Minister Thaksin Shinawatra claimed victory in his three month 'all-out campaign against drug trafficking'. The campaign included over 17,000 arrests and, disturbingly, the deaths of 2,274 people, most killed in 'extra-judicial executions'. Interior Minister Wan Mohammed Noor Matha worryingly warned that drug dealers would 'be put behind bars or even vanish without a trace. Who cares? They are destroying our country'. Thais may be Buddhists, but if you piss them off they'll burn your crop down.

Holland

Amsterdam has been the global Mecca of mashed-up marijuana mates for decades, but things are suddenly looking bleak for the Bulldog and other 'coffee shops' that sell weed in a loophole legality. The Netherlands has always been a progressive, if not controversial, state, being the first country to make cannabis available as a prescription drug in pharmacies for chronically ill patients. But all that looks set to change. In April 2004 the Dutch government decided to curb drugs tourism and sharpen cannabis policies amid European pressure from those party poopers in Brussels.

A trial will start in 2004 in the southern town of Maastricht, where the sale of soft drugs to foreigners will be banned. 'We want to end all aspects of drugs tourism, the fact that people come to the Netherlands to use soft drugs or to take them home,' said Justice Ministry spokesman and general bummer, Wim Kok.

The liberal Dutch laws on soft drugs, whose use is not allowed but condoned in a tacit acknowledgement that there are insufficient police to arrest all offenders, have been a thorn in the side to more tight-arsed European countries such as France, which abhors the return of hazy-eyed nationals by train.

The Justice Ministry will attack drugs tourism with international police co-operation and target large-scale hemp growing, as well as the 'criminal involvement' of so-called 'grow-shops' where people can buy seeds to grow their own pot. The Health Ministry, for its part, will study the possible health consequences of soft drugs with a high content of Tetrahydrocannabinol (THC), an active compound in cannabis. This study could lead to a reclassification of the high-THC content cannabis as a 'hard drug' – a complete reversal of the UK's recent downgrading of marijuana from a Class B drug to a Class C one.

Japan

The Land of the Rising Sun is not the first place your average cannabis tourist thinks of visiting. Japanese drug culture is unique in that the most popular illegal drug is not marijuana but speed (amphetamines). Cannabis is only the fifth most popular drug, after caffeine, alcohol, tobacco and illegal stimulants. Arguably, even paint thinner is more commonly abused than cannabis.

Above: 'You're only supposed to blow the bloody doors off!' The Brazilian Agriculture Minister does his bit for the 'War on Drugs' and the environment by exploding a seized bail of marijuana. D'oh!

Personal Highs:
The Wonder Weed!

In Max Jones and John Chilton's *Louis: The Louis Armstrong Story, 1900-71*, the great horn blower recounted his own experiences with marijuana in his own inimitable style.

'In 1931 we called ourselves vipers, which could have been anybody from all walks of life that smoked and respected gage. That was our cute little name for marijuana, and it was a misdemeanour in those days. Much different from the pressure and charges the law lays on a guy who smokes pot.... We always looked at pot as a sort of medicine, a cheap drunk and with much better thoughts than one that's full of liquor. But with the penalties that came, I for one had to put it down, though the respect for it (gage) will stay with me forever. I have every

reason to say these words and am proud to say them. From experience.

'... when Vic Berton [the top drummer] and I got busted together it was during our intermission at this big night club... Vic and I were blasting this joint – having lots of laughs and feeling good, enjoying each other's company. Just then two big healthy Dicks [detectives] came from behind a car nonchalantl and said to us, "We'll take the roach, boys." Vic and I said nothing. So one Dick stayed with me until I went into the Club and did my last show, he enjoyed it too. Because when he and I were on our way down to the police station we had a heart-to-heart talk. First words that he said to me were, "Armstrong, I am a big fan of yours and so is my family. We catch your programme every night over the radio," which I was glad to hear, especially coming from him. Ho ho... Immediately I said, "OK, let's ride." I also told him, "After all, I'm no criminal. I respect everybody and they respect me." "Hell," he said, "you ain't doing any more 'n' anybody's doing. It's when they get caught is when they're found out." I was so relaxed on the way down to the station until I forgot I was being busted.

'When we reached the police headquarters there were several officers... and the minute we came through the door they all recognized me right away. They too had been diggin' my music nightly over the radio.... They gave me one look and said, "What ta' hell are you doing here this time of night away from the club?" So we yakity yakity while I was being booked. That's one reason why we appreciated pot, as y'all calls it now. The warmth it always brought forth from the other person – especially the ones that it up a good stick of that shuzzit or gage... I spent nine days in the Downtown Los Angeles City Jail. Meantime the Chicago papers were all on the stands, with big headlines saying Louis Armstrong will have to serve six months for marijuana... the judge gave me a suspended sentence and I went to work that night – wailed just like nothing happened.

'As we always used to say, gage is more of a medicine than a dope. But with all the riggermaroo going on, no one can do anything about it. After all, the vipers during my heydays are way up there in age – too old to suffer those drastic penalties. So we had to put it down. But if we all get as old as Methuselah, our memories will always be of lots of beauty and warmth from gage. Well, that was my life and I don't feel ashamed at all. Mary Warner [marijuana], honey, you sure was good and I enjoyed you heap much. But the price got a little too high to pay (law wise). At first you was a "misdemeanour". But as the years rolled on you lost your misdo and got meaner and meaner. (Jailhousely speaking). Sooo, bye bye, I'll have to put you down, dearest.'

"Vic and I were blasting this joint – having lots of laughs and feeling good"

Above: A Japanese hemp grower checks her crop, which she uses to weave cloth.

However, wacky baccy has gained in popularity in Japan since the 1960s, especially amongst young people. In recent years the number of Japanese who visit foreign countries has risen dramatically and many bring back the love of smoking weed. As many as one in 50 Japanese, or over 2,000,000 people, have tried it.

Marijuana was officially criminalized in Japan by the post-World War II occupying US administration in 1948. Since then US-friendly Japanese governments have demonized marijuana, spreading propaganda that cannabis use can cause mental illness, mood swings, hallucinations and threats of violence to others. Most people in Japan believe that marijuana is a narcotic and are unaware that this 'dangerous' substance is the familiar crop that has been growing wild all over Japan for over 2,000 years.

Every year, over a million wild cannabis plants are allegedly destroyed by narcotics agents. In reality, the government's annual hemp eradication campaign is a bit of a joke, as it doesn't even take place during the hemp growing eason, but during the flowering season of opium poppies in May/June, making it more of an opium eradication campaign. In Hokkaido there are many stains of uncultivated hemp which are said to be fairly psychoactive (probably the northernmost in the world). People travel as far as Tokyo to harvest this wild weed, and every year a few are caught by police road blocks. Wild hemp grows well, from Okinawa to Hokkaido, as there's plenty of rainfall in the cool mountain climate. People grow it on wooded hillsides, in abandoned fields, hidden in bamboo or goldenrod, but increasingly home growers are using hydroponics, particularly in urban areas. Most of the home-cultivated weed is never sold and is only grown for personal use.

Cannabis has been part of Nippon's culture for centuries, and was used for everyday fibres and fabrics as well as for sacred rituals. Today, the Emperor still wears hemp clothes on some religious occasions. Regardless of the Emperor's hippie fashion sense, Japanese prison sentences for possession are similar to the UK's, with a maximum of five years, while dealing can get you seven years inside. However, again like the UK, most arrests for personal use result in suspended sentences or cautions. In 1995, 1,555 people were arrested under the Cannabis Control Act, a drop from the previous year's figure of 2,103. Typically police busts are exaggerated, with reports suggesting ¥5,000 per gram (£30/US$50) for marijuana or ¥6,000–8,000 (£36–48/US$65–85) per gram for hashish.

Realistically, normal street prices are much lower, around ¥2,000–3,000 per gram (£12–18 US$20 –$32), still almost twice USA prices. Since the current price of gold is about ¥1,000 (£6/US$10) per gram, Japanese marijuana is twice the price of gold, Acapulco or otherwise. It's estimated that there are about 100,000–700,000 cannabis users in Japan, about a tenth of those in most other industrialized countries. In a reverse trend of Morocco, hand-rolled cigarettes are rare in Japan, so most Japanese tokers use pipes instead of rolling papers. Pipes are small and easily concealed, just in case PC Yamamoto is on the prowl.

Japanese rarely even joke about marijuana, certainly when compared to the West (see Chronic Comedy). Yet, surprisingly, Japan didn't sign the letter to UN Secretary General Kofi Annan during the special UN plenary session on drugs in May 1998, so the field is wide open for educating politicians and voters. There has been a growing legalization movement since the early 1970s. Hemp stores are doing a good trade in smoking paraphernalia, spreading more balanced information on the value of the marijuana plant and the harm caused by prohibition, and the medical marijuana movement is beginning to bloom as well.

As with every country, when trying to score, herbalists should watch out, be careful, let it all come easy, and never, ever try to be smarter than the locals.

Have a happy trip.

Herbal Highs

Want to get wasted without worrying about the law beating down your door? The answer lies in herbal highs.

The herbal highs market took off in the US and UK in the mid-1990s, and has since expanded so that now many companies sell a variety of alternatives to marijuana. The effectiveness of these 'drugs' is open to massive debate. Hardcore stoners claim they are not a patch on cannabis, likening legal drugs to non-alcoholic lager. Others swear they produce similar, if not greater sensations. This is because many of them are much more hallucinogenic than weed. All herbals are made from a combination of naturally occurring plants and fungi and are packaged as either capsules, pills or as a loose pack for smoking, like tobacco.

Inhaling smoke is the fastest way to get a buzz, but herbs can also be taken in teas or as pills. However – like cooking with hash – it takes time to discover if whether too much or too little has been ingested, but once kicked in, herbal highs last much longer than marijuana.

The contents of these highs varies greatly, depending on what sort of rush the user is looking for. Wormwood is most famous for being the main active ingredient of the liqueur absinthe, the 'green fairy'. The herb has a spicy, bitter taste and contains thujones, chemicals that act on the brain in a similar way to cannabinoids. Wormwood also contains a toxin that, in high quantities, can bring on tremors, sleeplessness, paralysis, stomach problems and brain damage. But it also has narcotic-like effects, giving vivid dreams. For a while absinthe was outlawed in many countries, but is now legal in most of Europe.

A popular plant used in herbal smoking mixtures is *Salvia divinorum*, AKA holy sage. This soft-leafed Mexican plant contains psychoactive chemicals that have yet to be fully classified. Its powerful effects can be difficult to attain from smoking dried leaf, but can cause

Above: Marijuana's not the only way to get wasted. Amsterdam offers everything from Magic Mushrooms to Philosopher's Stones.

short-lived colourful hallucinations, lasting up to two hours. Unfortunately, some people also experience headaches and mild irritability, and it can even trigger latent psychological and mental problems.

High doses of damiana, a shrub found throughout Central and South America, can induce a mild sense of euphoria, lasting around on hour, with some fans claiming it's an aphrodisiac. But this might be offset by causing diarrhoea in others. Not quite the romantic evening you might have planned.

Other herbal ingredients include yohimbe – the bark and roots of an African tree; the Amazonian ayahuasca; the particularly nasty datura; and guarana. The latter is a South American berry containing a mild stimulant, guaranine, similar to caffeine. Smoking mixtures can also contain anything from skullcap mushrooms, peppermint, *lactuca virosa*, *artemesia vulgaris*, passion vine, lavender and scotch broom tops to sage, star of Bethlehem, St John's Wort, *turnera diffusa* and ground cardamom seeds.

Smoker's blends come with brand names such as Merlin's Blend, Spirit Walk and the chronic-inspired Tai Stix, Sativah and Wacky Weed. Capsules and pills have exotic names like Druids' Fantasy, Space Cadets, Bliss Extra and the blatantly titled aphrodisiac, Lust.

In 1997 the UK government tried to ban legal highs by classifying them under medicines, but soon realized that they'd have to enforce the laws in health food stores and consequently dropped the case. Therefore most herbal highs are not covered under the UK's Misuse of Drugs Act, but the Medicines Act warns that possession is only allowed for personal use, so no sharing with your friends. While some of these herbs do work, they are undoubtedly less predictable, and a few are far more dangerous, than a few tokes on a joint.

173

Chapter 6

Chronic Comedy

According to famous dope chef, Alice B. Toklas, marijuana brings on 'euphoria and brilliant storms of laughter...' So it's unsurprising that cannabis and stand-up comedy have been bedfellows for well over 50 years.

Chronic Comedy

Comedians are campaigners as well as entertainers, and many have been outspoken in their views of the weed – views that inevitably brought prosecution as well as praise.

Lenny Bruce

Bruce was the absent father of modern stand-up comedy. Before him, comedians told 'safe' racist or mother-in-law jokes. Bruce turned conventions on their head while messing with audiences' heads, waking them up to the truth behind governments, religion, drugs and sex. Because of his uncompromising approach, he made a lot of powerful enemies who were determined to destroy him.

Bruce was born Leonard Alfred Schneider on 13 October 1925 in Mineola, New York. According to Bruce's unreliable autobiography, *How To Talk Dirty And Influence People* (Playboy Press, 1965), he was introduced to hashish by a Turkish shipmate when he was a merchant seaman in the late 1940s. His first big break was in October 1948 on the Arthur Godfrey Talent Scouts show, and he spent the next few years touring comedy clubs across the country, refining his act. In the 1950s, he hung out with the hip, pot-smoking clique that congregated at 'The Castle', the stately home in Topanga Canyon of 'Hollywood hep-cat in residence', Lord Buckley.

Bruce was busted for possession of marijuana in 1956 along with his then-wife, Honey. He wa

Right: Lenny Bruce gets busted for the 56th time that day. When it wasn't for marijuana it was for saying cocksucker on stage.

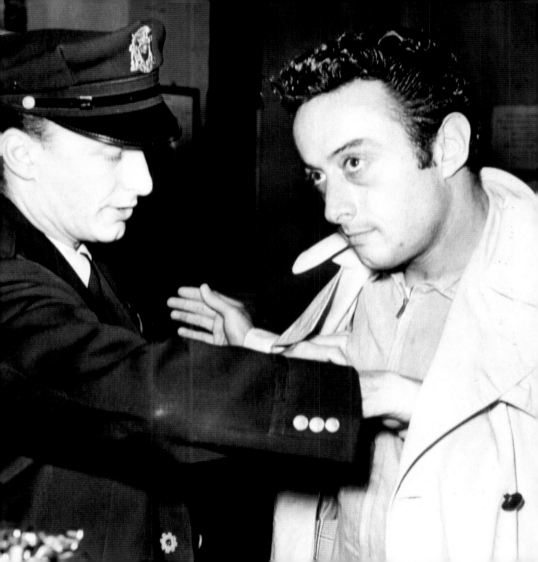

released, but she ended up serving two years after she broke parole. Despite this he once publicly, perhaps ironically, stated, 'I don't smoke pot, and I'm glad because then I can champion it without any special pleading. The reason I don't smoke pot is because it facilitates ideas and heightens sensations. And I get enough shit flying through my head without smoking pot.' Bruce began incorporating 'legalize pot' routines into his shows: 'Marijuana is rejected all over the world. Damned. In England heroin is all right for out-patents, but marijuana? They'll put your ass in jail. I wonder why that is?… the only reason could be: to Serve the Devil – Pleasure! Pleasure, which is a dirty word in Christian culture.' However, he was busted in Philadelphia on 29 September 1961 for possession of narcotics, but the charge was later dropped.

At his concerts Bruce sold copies of a home-made brochure, *Stamp Help Out*, which contained a hysterical pictorial and satirical thesis on 'The Pot Smokers', illustrated with 'actual photos of tortured marijuana-ites', most of whom were him. Because of various legal wrangles, nearly all copies of this landmark in stoned humour were promptly destroyed, and the few remaining are riddled with holes punched through Lenny's only extended discussion of marijuana. However, his priceless 'exposé of the dread narcotic, 'Cannabis sativa' appeared posthumously in *The Almost Unpublished Lenny Bruce*. Bruce wrote many sketches about grass, including a parody of a popular advert:

Whiney punter voice: 'I don't know what the hell it is, Bill, I've been smoking this pot all day and I still can't get high on it.'

Authoritative expert voice: 'What kind are you smoking?'

WP: 'Well, all marijuana's the same, isn't it?'

AE: 'That's the mistake a lot of people make!'

Famously arrested at the Jazz Workshop in San Francisco on 4 October 1961 for violating the California obscenity code for saying the word 'cocksucker' on stage, he was again acquitted. The following year he was banned from performing in Australia. Bruce was now being targeted by the police, who secretly taped his gigs as evidence. In retaliation he started secretly recording his trials. He was arrested a second time for possessing narcotics (he was using heroin), and for using the phrase 'Where is that dwarf motherfucker?' at the Troubador Theatre in Hollywood.

The subsequent obscenity trial in San Francisco was a landmark fight for freedom of speech, but bankrupted Bruce. 'If you can't say "Fuck", you can't say, "Fuck the government",' railed the unrepentant comedian. After being yet again acquitted, Bruce's last performance was in June 1966 at the famed Filmore Auditorium in San Francisco. Two months later he died from a morphine overdose at his Hollywood home. Allen Ginsberg, the Beat poet proponent of pot, spoke at Bruce's memorial service, and his legacy lives on in songs such as REM's 'End of the World'

('Lenny Bruce is not afraid') and Simon & Garfunkel's 'A Simple Desultory Philippic' ('And I learned the truth from Lenny Bruce').

George Carlin *(left)*

Bruce's mantle was handed down to up-and-coming comedian, George Carlin. In 1960, Carlin teamed with a young newscaster named Jack Burns and began doing a comedy act at small clubs and folk rooms. Burns and Carlin were soon discovered by Lenny Bruce. 'Lenny got us a contract with a major agency, which was incredible,' Carlin remembered. 'I mean, we'd been comedians for a month and a half when we got booked into the Playboy Club circuit purely on the basis of Lenny going to bat for us.'

Carlin had always been a toker: 'In my neighbourhood – West 121st Street in New York, "white Harlem" – there were only two drugs: smack and marijuana. By the time I was thirteen, some friends and I were using marijuana fairly regularly. The *Reefer Madness* myth was still very strong then, but I'd been into jazz and those lyrics included so many casual references to pot that it was completely demystified for me. Heroin, forget it. In my neighbourhood, I could see what heroin did firsthand, and I was definitely afraid of that number.'

Burns and Carlin split in 1962, and the latter's career continued its ascent on TV. Unknown to Carlin during this 'straight' period was a prediction made by Lenny Bruce, that Carlin would one day assume Bruce's throne as king of the social comics.

Personal Highs:
Mid-Life Pot Convert

Lester Grinspoon, MD, is on the faculty (emeritus) of the Harvard Medical School in the Department of Psychiatry.

He's studied cannabis since 1967, and has published two books on the subject: *Marihuana Reconsidered* (1971) and *Marihuana, the Forbidden Medicine* (1997). He's also set up www.marijuana-uses.com to record people's personal experiences with the wacky baccy. Here's one of his own.

'[After two initially disappointing experiences with marijuana] Finally, on our third attempt, we were able to reach the promised high. Our awareness of having at last crossed the threshold arrived gradually. The first thing I noticed, within a few minutes of smoking, was the music; it was

Sgt. Pepper's Lonely Hearts Club Band. This music was not unfamiliar to me, as it was a favourite of my children, who constantly filled the house with the sound of the Beatles, the Grateful Dead and other popular rock bands of the time. On that evening… it was for me a rhythmic implosion, a fascinating new musical experience! It was the opening of new musical vistas, which I have, with the help of my sons, continued to explore to this very day. A year later, I related this story to John Lennon and Yoko Ono, with whom I was having dinner. I told John of this experience and how cannabis appeared to make it possible for me to "hear" his music for the first ime… John was quick to reply that I had experienced only one facet of what marijuana could do for music, that he thought it could be very helpful for composing and making music as well as listening to it.

'… Betsy and I and another couple were standing in the kitchen in a circle, each of us in turn taking bites out of a Napoleon [a puff pastry dessert]. There was much hilarity as each bite forced the viscous material between the layers to move laterally and threaten to drip on the floor… but the most memorable part of the kitchen experience was the taste of the Napoleon. None of us had ever, "in our whole lives", eaten such an exquisite Napoleon! It was gradually dawning on me that something unusual was happening; could it be that we were experiencing our first cannabis high?

'We drove home very cautiously… time passed even more slowly between our arrival and our going to bed, but once we did, we knew with certainty that we had finally been able to achieve a marijuana high. And that marked the beginning of the experiential facet of my cannabis era, a development that furthered my education about the many uses of this remarkable drug.

'I was forty-four years old in 1972 when I experienced this first marijuana high. Because I have found it both so useful and benign, I have used it ever since. I have used it as a recreational drug, as a medicine, and as an enhancer of some capacities… I cannot possibly convey the breadth of things it helps me to appreciate, to think about, to gain new insights into… Betsy and I are gradually being given the opportunity to explore another dimension of the ways in which cannabis can be valuable; we are discovering its usefulness in the task of achieving reconciliation with the ageing process, including coming to terms with the inevitable physical and emotional aches, deficits and losses. Cannabis also enhances our appreciation of the time we have… to enjoy our children, grandchildren and friends, literature, music and travel, and our daily walks in the New England woods. Of still more importance, it helps us to realize the wisdom of Robert Browning's words, "Grow old along with me! The best is yet to be…"'

Beautiful.

"I was 44 years old when I experienced this first marijuana high."

'Apparently, Lenny told that to a lot of people,' said Carlin in 1982, 'but he never said it to me, and I didn't hear it until years later. Which is probably fortunate. It's difficult enough for a young person to put his soul on the line in front of a lot of drunken people without having that hanging over his head, too.' Then, one night in 1970 in Las Vegas, something happened to Carlin. While entertaining a business convention he threw out all his safe material and started attacking everything from religion to corporate greed. Those audience members who didn't walk out tried to storm the stage and punch the comedian. A new, socially conscious, counterculture Carlin was born.

Like his former mentor, Carlin also got into trouble for swearing, with his 'Seven Words You Can't Say on the Radio or Television' skit, which was deemed by the Supreme Court as 'Indecent but not Obscene'. Thirty years later, in December 2003, a US Congressman introduced a bill to outlaw the broadcast of Carlin's seven 'dirty words'.

In 1975 Carlin was the first guest host on NBC's *Saturday Night Live*, the ground-breaking sketch show that launched the careers of Dan Aykroyd, John Belushi and Bill Murray, among others. Then Carlin was hit by a massive cocaine addiction and heart attack (just like comedian, friend and fellow toker, Richard Pryor) and disappeared for five years. He re-emerged in 1982, and in a lengthy *Playboy* interview revealed his continued love of marijuana. 'I was a stonehead for thirty years. I'd wake up in the morning, and if I couldn't decide whether I wanted to smoke a joint or not, I'd smoke a joint to figure it out. And I stayed high all day long. When people asked me, "Do you get high to go onstage?" I could never understand the question. I mean, I'd been high since eight that morning. Going onstage had nothing to do with it.' He continued, 'Grass probably helped me as much as it hurt me. Especially as a performer. When you're high, it's easy to kid yourself about how clever certain mediocre pieces of material are. But, on the other hand, pot opens windows and doors that you may not be able to get through any other way. Being a very bound-up, Irish Catholic tight-assholed person, I've often thought that whatever negative effects pot had on me, it probably saved me from being an alcoholic and a complete fucking brainless idiot by the time I was twenty-five.'

In 1989 Carlin revived his career, playing Rufus in *Bill and Ted's Excellent Adventure* and the sequel, *Bill and Ted's Bogus Journey* (1991). In 1999 he starred alongside the modern-day super-stoners Jay and Silent Bob in *Dogma,* and again in *Jay and Silent Bob Strike Back* (2001). 'Now, there's no question that it's sort of fun to get high,' reminisced Carlin. 'The ritual was very important to me: cleaning the pot, rolling the pot – I was never a pipe or bong man. That's California stuff. I was an Eastern roller. My daughter had to teach me to use a water pipe, and I'd still fuck it up every time. To me, smoking pot meant sitting with a newspaper on my legs, rolling the seeds down, pulling the twigs out, and inally producing a perfectly cylindrical, absolutely wonderful joint that you either locked at both ends or pinched off, or pinched at one end and left open at the other.' Having made riends with the director Kevin 'Silent Bob' Smith, Carlin also starred in *Jersey Girl* in 2004 in a ole written for him. As he's got older, Carlin's mellow demeanour has become a more natural state: 'To my surprise, my marijuana use has been tapering off steadily. As we speak, I haven't had a joint in two months.'

Bill Hicks

Hicks was cut from the same cloth as Bruce and Carlin, yet was even more militant regarding cannabis and other drugs: 'Not only do I think pot should be legalized, it should be mandatory.'

The Texan-born 'Prince of Darkness' was destined to be more than just a stand up comedian. He was a social satirist, political commentator and philosopher. At 13, he'd sneak out of his suburban house to hustle his way onto open-mike nights at local comedy clubs. In two brief decades, Hicks worked his way up the sweat-stained comedy ladder to national exposure on *The Tonight Show, Late Show with David Letterman* and an HBO cable special. *Rolling Stone* named him 'hot stand-up' of 1993. He was the hit of the 1990 and 1991 *Just for Laughs* comedy festivals in Montreal. Hicks frequently did over 250 gigs a year, as he tried to reach as many people as possible to spread the truth, like Bruce before him.

'I've had some killer times on drugs,' he said, promoting their legalization. 'But not all drugs are good… some of them are great!' He regularly picked out the irony of the US government's drug policies: 'George Bush says, "We're losing the War On Drugs". Well, what does that tell you? That there's a war on, and the people that are winning it are on drugs.'

He continued, 'They tell you that pot smoking makes you unmotivated. Lie! When you're high, you can do everything you normally do just as well. You just realize it's not worth the fucking effort.' Hicks would often rant and rave about the hypocrisy in the world, leaving no sacred cows. 'Why is marijuana against the law? It grows naturally on our planet. Doesn't the idea of making nature against the law seem a bit paranoid? To make it illegal is kind of like saying God made a mistake.'

Despite a big following in the UK, Hicks never made it big in his home country. At his final show he went out with, 'This is the material, by the way, that has kept me virtually anonymous in America for the past fifteen years. Gee, I wonder why we're hated the world over? Look at these fat Americans in the front row – "Why doesn't he just hit fruit with a hammer?" Folks, I could have done that, walked around being a millionaire and franchising myself, but no, I had to have this weird thing about trying to illuminate the collective unconscious and help humanity. Fucking moron.'

He was diagnosed with pancreatic cancer and died in 1994. Hicks was possibly the most important stand-up comedian since Lenny Bruce, but 'I don't *ever* remember Bill being big on Lenny Bruce,' recalled Hicks's best friend Kevin Booth. 'I think one of the cool things is, in San Francisco, John Magnison, who produced a lot of Lenny Bruce stuff, approached Bill after the show and said, "You know, I hear all the time, like, hey, you gotta go see this guy, he's the new Lenny Bruce." Yeah, he hears that about various people all the time, and he always goes and sees them and is always disappointed, but when he went and saw Bill, he was just blown away. When the history books are all said and done, you know, Lenny's not really going to be remembered as a comic, and I don't really think Bill Hicks will be either.'

Hicks's legend is now so powerful that Stephen Pound, MP, stood up in the House of Commons and said, '…this House notes with sadness the tenth anniversary of the death of Bill Hicks, on 26 February 1994, at the age of thirty-three; recalls his assertion that his words would be a bullet in the heart of consumerism, capitalism and the American Dream; and mourns the passing of one of the few people who may be mentioned as being worthy of inclusion with Lenny Bruce in any list of unflinching and painfully honest political philosophers.'

Denis Leary *(above right)*

One of Hicks' contemporaries was Denis Leary, who was born and raised in Worcester, Massachusetts, the son of Irish immigrants. His

cousin, Conan O'Brien, the late night chat show host, once joked on his TV show that 'Fifty-four per cent of Canadian teenagers use marijuana. The other forty-six per cent grow it.' Leary spent the early part of his life acting and writing for magazines, and started doing stand-up comedy. In 1990, he and his pregnant wife, Ann, flew to London to perform in the BBC's *Paramount City*. That weekend, Ann's waters roke, and their planned weekend trip became a stay of months. Leary, faced with not much to do, started writing a one-man comedy act. He brought friends in from the States and they wrote songs for the show.

Denis Leary, with Chris Phillips and Adam Roth on guitar, performed *No Cure For Cancer* at the 1991 Edinburgh Festival. The show won the Critic's Award and the BBC Festival Recommendation, thanks to his witty observations of stoner culture: 'For years pot was just joints, and then bongs came out and bongs were OK too, but then bongs weren't good enough for some people,' Leary would rant. Remember that friend in high school who wanted to make bongs out of everything? Making bongs out of apples and oranges and shit? Come in one day and find your friend going, "Hey! Look man, I made a bong outta my head! Put the pot in this ear and take it outta this one! Good! Take a hit!" Then they got one of those big giant bongs that you gotta start up like a motorcycle. "Put the pot in!" Kids are driving their bongs down FDR Drive. "Pull the bong over, man, I wanna do a hit. Pull it over!"'

In 1992 the show moved to America, spawning a book, CD and videotape. Leary became an overnight sensation with skits like: What was the problem with just smoking a joint, eating a couple of Twinkies, and going to sleep? Was that a problem? They say marijuana leads to other drugs. No it doesn't, it leads to fucking carpentry. That's the problem, folks. People

getting high going, "Wow man, this box would make an excellent bong! This guy's head would make an excellent bong!"'

Leary had been friends with Bill Hicks, but when Hicks heard *No Cure For Cancer* he accused Leary of stealing his material and ended the friendship. Kevin Booth, Hicks's album producer and best friend since high school, recalled, 'Well, I know he was annoyed by Denis Leary... we had just finished doing the *Marble Head Johnson* music album and [Hicks] was performing alongside Denis Leary. Bill went somewhere with Denis and handed him this demo tape. The next thing you know, Denis puts out an album of musical comedy. This is already after the kind of feelings that got created because of the smoking guy in the jacket.' Booth continued, '... these guys are two kinds of people, people that are evolving ideas and then people that are just stealing ideas, and definitely Leary was one who was stealing... I just know that when Bill and I were driving to go see the Branch Davidian siege, he had just bought the Leary album and put it on and was just playing it and just seething, seething in a way of like, "Great, this guy is selling a zillion copies on Warner Brothers, doing all of my ideas and material."'

Leary started doing savage and hilarious monologue links for MTV as the chain-smoking 'Nicotine Fiend', and since then has concentrated on his acting career in Hollywood movies such as *Demolition Man, Wag the Dog* and *Ice Age*.

"Everyone should eat hashish, but only once."

Salvador Dali

"**Whatever I'm already doing becomes enhanced when I smoke pot. It can also be demotivating, because if I'm not doing anything and I smoke a joint, it enhances just sitting in a chair. Then I don't even want to get up to change a record.**"

Chrissie Hynde

Robin Williams

'The funniest man alive' is no stranger to drugs: 'Reality is just a crutch for people who can't cope with drugs'. Although clean and sober now, back in the Seventies he was a demon user. For a while, like many performers, he'd been using alcohol and drugs heavily, including grass and in particular cocaine. He was good friends with John Belushi (Saturday Night Live, The Blues Brothers), and the two would play 'cocaine chicken', where two people start at each end of a line of coke and race to the middle. Belushi always won. Williams got loaded with Belushi the day he overdosed, although Williams wasn't at the Chateau Marmont Hotel when Belushi actually died. Robert De Niro was also there that day, and both testified before a grand jury.

Williams eventually kicked the habit, Belushi's death being the wake-up call – 'Cocaine is God's way of telling you you're making too much money' – and he went on to win a Grammy in 1986 for his Live At The Met comedy LP. At the Met he joked, 'Then there's those people who get their pets stoned. Don't get your dog stoned. He's not that high on the food chain to begin with. He's only just learnt to lick his balls, leave him alone.'

Unlike many comedians who praise the 'erb, Williams's routines often have a tinge of

Left: Robin Williams joked about being stoned and pulled over by the police, 'Eat everything in the ashtray!'

bitterness about them: 'Marijuana enhances many things – taste, colour, sensations – but you are certainly not fucking empowered.' Since his stand-up days Williams has gone on to become one of the most well-known actors in Hollywood, adding serious dramatic roles to his ever expanding repertoire. But he remains serious about his comedy: 'You're only given a little spark of madness,' he said. 'You mustn't lose that madness.'

Richard Pryor

'Madness' was something Richard Pryor wrestled with all his life. Most comedians' lives seem to be tainted with a bit of misfortune which makes their humour better, but Pryor's was a tragedy of Greek proportions. Born in Peoria, Illinois, Pryor was the son of a prostitute and often watched his mother turn tricks. He dropped out of school at 14 and began shining shoes and working in pool halls and strip joints until 1958, when he joined the army. He was jailed after he stabbed a white recruit who was fighting with a black soldier.

After various menial jobs Pryor began working as a comic in 1963. 'In Peoria there was this club, The Brown Club. I went and asked the owner for a job playing the piano,' reminisced Pryor. 'When I played and sang – I tried to sound all smooth and Steve Gormez-like, and he saw I was bullshitting him, 'cause I never played the piano before – he laughed his ass off and told me, "You're a funny motherfucker, you should be a comedian." He hired me as a comedian, and I told lame-ass jokes with my friend Sonny Stetson punctuating my tired old jokes with the drum. That's how I started.'

Like any other performer, Richard Pryor was influenced by the comedians who came before him. One factor that profoundly affected Pryor was the styling of Lenny Bruce. Pryor greatly respected his bravery in performing controversial material on stage and believed that Bruce's 'Lima, Ohio' is the funniest comedy routine ever made.

Pryor's initial goal was to appeal to white audiences, and he became more popular than Bill Cosby, with early material that was straight-laced and for the whole family. That soon changed. One night in the middle of a routine, like Carlin, he had an epiphany, said 'What the fuck am I doing here?' and walked off. He started doing racier material, reclaimed the phrase 'nigger' for blacks and was banned from many clubs, but soon started a brand-new following.

Pryor first toked marijuana in 1960, and during the birth of his daughter Elizabeth Anne, he was in jail for marijuana possession. Unfortunately the weed unlocked his addictive personality. Pryor moved onto cocaine in the mid-1960s, and by the Seventies he was freebasing it. Despite the downward spiral of his personal life (being married five times and shooting wife Deborah McGuire's Mercedes with a .357 Magnum to prevent her from leaving), his stand-up routine albums won him plaudits, five Grammys and an Emmy.

Pryor suffered his first heart attack while high and in the middle of a threesome. He was to have two more, the last in 1991.

Infamously in 1980, while freebasing cocaine, Pryor doused himself with cognac and set himself on fire in what he later called a suicide attempt. While on fire, he ran from his home through the streets. He spent more than six weeks in the hospital recovering from third-degree burns that covered over 50 per cent of his body.

In 1986, Pryor was diagnosed as having multiple sclerosis. Despite going through rehab and giving up hard drugs, he stayed faithful to the ganja, using it to ease the symptoms of his MS. He became a vocal proponent for the use of medical marijuana, and in 1999 lobbied Congress in a letter alongside Susan Sarandon, Woody Harrelson and Harvard scientist Stephen Jay Gould.

At Pryor's prize-giving for the 1999 inaugural Mark Twain Prize for American Humour, Robin Williams said, 'Richard Pryor is an alchemist who can turn the darkest pain into the deepest comedy. [He] doesn't go for the jugular, he goes straight for the aorta.' Despite all the tragedy in his life Pryor remains an optimistic survivor. As he succinctly puts it, 'I ain't dead yet, motherfucker!'

Right: Richard Pryor was so wasted in the Eighties he starred in *Superman 3*.

Cannabis Comix Capers

Ever since the heady hippie days of the Sixties, comix and pot-smoking have been inextricably linked. The underground comix revolution that started in San Francisco focused on sex, rock and roll and, of course, drugs. And it is a tradition that's been kept up to this very day.

Back in 1968, a young toker from Texas, Gilbert Shelton, created the most enduring and iconic stoner comic characters, The Fabulous Furry Freak Brothers. The trio of Phineas Freak, Fat Freddy and Freewheelin' Franklin remain beloved heroes of hemp to this day, and their adventures remain in print over 35 years later. Shelton's success inspired many other cartoonists to get

into chronic comics, including Robert Crumb and Dave Sheridan, the latter with his Dealer McDope (1969), a prolific pot peddler. The Sixties and Seventies saw numerous one-shots and miniseries pop up relating to dope, including

Right: Issue #5 of Gilbert Shelton's infamous comic, soon to be an animated film…

s Marijuana Multiplier by Larry Todd
Jay Lynch's *The Great Marijuana*
72).

m the obvious references to grass in
d comix, there were subliminal ones
3 into mainstream comics, whether
or not. 'I never smoked marijuana,'
ee, the co-creator of classic Marvel
acters the Fantastic Four, Spider-
credible Hulk and the X-Men. 'When
der-Man's girlfriend Mary Jane [in
s only after a while that somebody
pretty nervy giving her the
marijuana!" I had no idea that's
the naive Lee confessed in *Maxim*

vent on to appear in director Kevin
ats (1995), the latter's homage to
ing. The film also starred Smith's
creations, Jay and Silent Bob,
eared in his debut movie *Clerks*
soon developed a cult following,
until 1997 that their stoner
er-egos, Bluntman and Chronic,
ed in *Chasing Amy*, in which the
ne are turned into a successful
written and drawn by Holden
d by Ben Affleck) which is
a movie in *Jay and Silent Bob*
2001. Bluntman and Chronic
joints and the stoner way against
reatens their native Tri-Town.
t their own comic in the real

world in a special drawn by Mic!
Oeming, Pat Garrahy and Mike
Silent Bob got their own comic i
prequel to Smith's 1999 movie *L*
miniseries was written by Smith a
British artist Duncan Fegredo.

Other recent cannabis comics in
Art Penn's 1993 adaptation of the
propaganda film, *Hemp for Victory*
made in 1942, when the Japanese
supply of Manila hemp. The US g
immediately distributed 18,000kg
cannabis seeds to farmers from W
Kentucky and made them attend so
Department of Agriculture's film. Pe
lovingly recreates the movie's messa

Meanwhile, in the UK the Scottis
Electric Soup (1989–93) and its su
Northern Lightz (named after the p
cannabis strain) have continued to
flaming joint of dope comix. Both t
the Shelton-inspired MacBam Broth
Pudden and Tam (the Mad Mental A
were created by Dave Alexander an
essentially a Scottish Freak Brothers
similar cult status. Other classic strip
superheroics of 'The Astounding Ga
'Cronic the Budbarian' and the sava
[Howard] 'Marks and Lennon, Dece

Even Tank Girl, that early Nineties
was extremely partial to the odd tok
Hewlett and Alan Martin's creation o
appeared in *Deadline* magazine in 1

a tank-driving, gun-toting, kangaroo-snogging, joint-smoking eruption of irreverence and irrelevance, and she took the world by storm, advertising Wrangler jeans and becoming a lesbian role model. But despite the apparently shallow storylines, there was an intelligent undercurrent where Hewlett and Martin paid tribute to the pot-smoking beatnik pioneers, Jack Kerouac and Allen Ginsberg, particularly in the storyline 'Blue Helmet'. In fact *Tank Girl* was crammed full of pot-smoking hippy 'guest stars', from Jimi Hendrix to Wyatt and Billy, the blissed-out bikers from *Easy Rider*. All *Tank Girl*'s characters got regularly wasted, and despite a dreadfully sanitized 1995 movie adaptation, continued to do so on the big screen.

Other UK titles, such as 2001's *Black Eye*, took a more young, black, urban look at weed. Positioning itself as a black *Viz* humour-type title, *Black Eye*'s publisher, Bobby Joseph, created a whole raft of modern stoneheads, including Reverend Roland Reed, 'He smokes 'nuff weed', Big Val… Yardie Gal and stoner superheroes Mighty Rastafarian and Boy Irie.

Left: Kevin Smith's creations Jay and Silent Bob as their super stoner alter egos, Bluntman and Chronic. The dope duo finally got their own comic drawn by Michael Avon Oeming and Pat Garrahy.

Chapter 7

Cannabis Cocktails

Cooking with grass or hash is well documented, but not many people know that it's also possible to make cannabis drinks as well. THC, the main psychoactive chemical of cannabis, is soluble in fats, oils and alcohol, but not in water. One way to make a drinkable form of cannabis is to infuse it in a strong spirit – a reasonably sweet drink with a high percentage of alcohol is recommended, such as a fruit schnapps.

Cannabis Cocktails

To construct a cocktail, you need to make a tincture, a liquid form of marijuana. This is easier than it initially sounds. To make a tincture you will need:

- Marijuana leaves and/or buds, or resin
- Alcohol (ethyl, brandy, flavoured schnapps or similar – 40–70% proof minimum)
- Muslin, fine sieve or coffee filter
- Funnel
- Glass bottle with screw lid

1 Take 3–5 parts of alcohol. The tincture can sometimes taste a bit bitter, so it is best to mix it with a strongly flavoured alcohol, rather than vodka or plain ethyl.

2 Grind up 1 part cannabis leaves and/or flowers e.g. 22g (¾oz) marijuana to 90ml/3fl oz alcohol. It's better to use grass rather than resin, as this tends to be purer and easier to filter out the solid that remains after extraction. Before you add the alcohol, soak the grass in warm water overnight, to remove any watersoluble impurities but not any of that precious THC. After soaking, drain

off the excess water, place the residue in an airtight jar and pour in the alcohol.

3 Keep in a dark and cool place for about 10 days, shaking the jar daily. Filter using a sieve; if using resin, filter through a coffee filter. You should repeat this process at least once, but the tincture will improve and strengthen if you do it again. Store the green/brown-coloured tincture somewhere dark and cold. Most of the THC will have been absorbed within a week, but connoisseurs leave it for a year or more. The tincture can be drunk neat or dissolved in a drink or food.

A little practice will let you find your personal favourite flavours and strengths. The standard 'jigger' or 'shot' in the recipes below is 15ml (½fl oz). As with cooking with cannabis, you should always err on the side of caution when it comes to the strengths and quantities. Note that excessive drinking of cannabis tinctures can have nasty short-term psychological side-effects, such as panic attacks, so proceed with caution.

Jamaican Ganja Juice

15ml (½fl oz) of
gin/cannabis tincture
30ml (1fl oz) melon liqueur
60ml (2fl oz) of
tropical fruit juice
Cracked ice

Combine gin/cannabis
tincture, melon liqueur, fruit
juice and ice in shaker.
Shake until frosty.
Pour into large goblet.
Garnish with plenty of fruit
in case of munchies.

Stoner Surprise

15ml (½fl oz) of dark rum/
cannabis tincture
30ml (1fl oz) Jamaican rum
30ml (1fl oz) light rum
30ml (1fl oz) lemon
or lime juice
4 dashes passion fruit
or orange juice
4 dashes of apricot brandy
4 dashes of cherry brandy
cracked ice
fresh fruit such as pineapple,
kiwi fruit, papaya or paw paw,
cherries to garnish

Half fill blender with cracked ice.
Add dark rum/cannabis tincture, Jamaica
rum, light rum, lemon or lime juice, passion
fruit or orange juice, apricot brandy and
cherry brandy and blend well.
Pour into large glass.
Decorate with a fresh cannabis leaf,
if desired, and garnish with plenty of
fruit in case of munchies.

**A range of truly 'mind blowing'
cocktails – (left to right) – a Stoner
Surprise, a Lean Green Mean
Machine and a Pot Colada.**

Lean Green Mean Machine *(left)*

15ml (½fl oz) of light rum/cannabis tincture
30ml (1fl oz) melon liqueur
30ml (1fl oz) vodka
cracked and cubed ice

lemonade
piece of watermelon
1 cherry

Combine rum/cannabis tincture, melon liqueur, vodka and cracked ice in shaker. Shake until frosty. Pour into large goblet over cubed ice. Fill with lemonade. Garnish with watermelon and cherry. Serve with straw.

Pot Colada

15ml (½fl oz) of light rum/cannabis tincture
30ml (1fl oz) pineapple juice
30ml (1fl oz) coconut milk
15ml (½fl oz) cream
1 maraschino cherry
piece of pineapple
1 hollowed-out coconut (or large glass)
cracked ice

Combine ice with light rum/cannabis tincture, pineapple juice, coconut milk and cream in shaker. Strain into hollowed-out coconut or large glass. Decorate with a fresh cannabis leaf if desired. If you have any coconuts left, try turning them into home-made bongs. The coconut milk will act as a filter giving a cool, thick smoke.

Marijuana Sour

15ml (½fl oz) of melon liqueur/cannabis tincture
60ml (2fl oz) lemon juice
1 egg white
2 melon balls
1 maraschino cherry
cracked ice

Combine melon liqueur/cannabis tincture,
lemon juice, egg white and ice in shaker.
Shake until frosty. Strain into glass and
garnish with melon balls and cherry.

Blasted Cow *(far right)*

15ml (½fl oz) of light rum/cannabis tincture
45ml (1½fl oz) cream
30ml (1fl oz) creme de banana
dash of Grenadine
grated nutmeg
3 slices of banana
cracked ice

Combine ice with cream, light rum/cannabis
tincture, crème de banana and Grenadine
in shaker and mix well.
Strain into cocktail glass.
Sprinkle with a finely grated mix of
hashish and nutmeg.

Sensimilla Lady

15ml (½fl oz) of Tequila/cannabis tincture
30ml (1fl oz) of melon liqueur
90ml (3fl oz) of grapefruit juice
slice of lemon
slice of lime
2 coloured cherries
cracked and cubed ice

Combine melon liqueur, Tequila/cannabis
tincture, grapefruit juice and cracked ice
in a shaker. Shake until frosty.
Pour over cubed ice in highball glass.
Decorate with slice of lemon and lime
and cherries.

More tea, vicar?
You can also make a nice herbal tea
with 0.5g (¹⁄₃₂oz) of dried cannabis
flowers in 500ml (1pt) of boiling water.
Add milk to taste.

**Capable of 'downing' an elephant at forty
paces – *(left to right)* – a Marijuana Sour, a
Blasted Cow and a Sensimilla Lady.**

what to do when you're too stoned!

**You can't overdose on cannabis, but smoking too much i[s]
something most tokers have experienced. Feelings of
paranoia and 'The Fear' can sometimes be overwhelming[.]
Here's what to do when it doesn't feel like fun anymore...**

• Stay Calm

Your mind will tell you that something is wrong
and induce feelings of panic, the more you panic
the more your brain will worry about what's
happening and you can get trapped in a negative
feedback loop. As soon as these feelings occur
tell yourself this is normal, and you're just too
stoned. The more you relax, the quicker the
feeling will go away.

• Talk to a Friend

Tell someone you're not enjoying this and
hopefully they will talk you down. Someone
more experienced at smoking is best – don't

ring your most pious friend, they'll just make
you feel guilty and more paranoid.

• Have a Cold Drink

Your mouth will be pretty dry, adding to your
brain's concerns, so get yourself a good cold drink
with plenty of ice. Cordial works best; blackcurrant
is good, but nothing beats a glass of lemon.

• Avoid Alcohol

When you're really stoned alcohol just enhances
the problem, so avoid trying to cancel out the
feelings of one with the other.

• Watch Cartoons

The key to riding out the feeling is taking your mind off it. The bright colours, quick-fire comedy and sheer off-the-wall nature of animation is perfect for diverting your attention without the need to focus too hard.

• Have a Shower

Stand or sit under a shower. It doesn't have to be cold, in fact warm is better. The feeling will divert the brain from its stoned paranoia, but also running water produces negative ions, a proven way of promoting relaxation.

• Go to Sleep

If your mind is racing, this is one of the hardest things to do. But try lying in a dark room, continually telling yourself that there's nothing actually wrong with you, and hopefully sleep will take over. You will wake up feeling fine and events of the previous evening will seem like a bad dream.

• Don't be Tempted to Drive

You may find a desire to leave where you are, under no circumstances should you drive. Although there is still debate about whether people can drive safely when stoned, all of it is insignificant should you actually have a serious accident. Stay where you are and come down.

205

Chapter 8

A Trip Through Time

Cannabis has been around longer than mankind, but over the centuries how did the 'holy herb' become the 'demon weed'?

6000–4000BC: The earliest known fabric is woven from hemp, and cannabis seeds are used for food in China.

2737BC: The first written record of cannabis use is made in the Chinese pharmacopoeia of Shen Nung. The father of Chinese medicine calls it a 'superior' herb.

1200–800BC: The Hindu sacred text *Atharva-veda* cites cannabis as 'Sacred Grass', and lists it amongst the five sacred plants of India. It is used medicinally and ritually as an offering to Shiva.

550BC: The Persian prophet Zoroaster writes the *Zend-Avesta*, a sacred text which lists more than 10,000 medicinal plants. Top of the list is hemp.

500BC: The Scythians introduce hemp into Northern Europe.

450BC: The Greek historian Herodotus records, in *The Histories*, Scythians throwing hemp onto heated stones under canvas,: '...as it burns, it smokes like incense, and the smell of it makes them drunk'.

First century AD: The Chinese begin making paper from hemp and mulberry.

400: Hemp cultivation is recorded for the first time in England.

512: The first botanical drawing of cannabis appears in the codex *Constantinopolitanus*, a contemporary materia medica.

800: The Islamic prophet Mohammed permits cannabis use, but forbids alcohol.

1090–1156: In Khorasan, Persia, Hassan-ibn Sabah, the 'Old Man of the Mountain', recruits followers to commit assassinations under the influence of hashish.

1150: Moslems use cannabis to start Europe's first paper mill. Hemp is the primary ingredient for papermaking for the next 850 years.

1200–1300: Arab traders bring cannabis to the Mozambique coast of Africa.

1379: In Egypt, Emir Soudon Sheikhouni prohibits cannabis consumption amongst the poor, destroys the crops, and has offenders' teeth pulled out.

1484: Pope Innocent VIII labels cannabis as an unholy sacrament of the Satanic mass and issues a ban on cannabis medicines.

1526: The first recorded use of hashish in Afghanistan.

1545–55: Spanish conquistadors bring cannabis cultivation to South America.

1563: Elizabeth I orders landowners with 60 acres or more to grow cannabis or face a £5 fine.

1564: King Philip of Spain orders cannabis to be grown throughout his empire, from Argentina to Oregon.

1619: The British Jamestown colony of Virginia makes hemp cultivation mandatory; most of the newly founded colonies follow suit. Farmers face jail terms for not growing hemp. Some colonies allow farmers to pay taxes with cannabis hemp.

1753: *Cannabis sativa* classified by Swedish botanist Carolus Linnaeus.

1776: Patriot wives and mothers spin thread from hemp fibres to clothe George Washington's troops.

28 June 1776: The first and second drafts of the Declaration of Independence are written on Dutch hemp paper. The final draft, signed by the Founders, is copied onto animal parchment.

1783: The French biologist Jean Baptiste de Lamarck classifies another species of cannabis: *Cannabis indica.*

1798: After invading Egypt, Napoleon bans his troops from buying and using cannabis. The prohibition fails, and samples are taken back to France.

1841: Psychologist Jacques-Joseph Moreau de Tours documents physical and mental benefits of cannabis after experimenting with animals and human mental patients.

1841: In his essay 'On the Preparation of the Indian Hemp or Ganja', the Irish physician Dr William O'Shaughnessy introduces cannabis to Western science.

1843: *Le Club de Hachichins* ('Hashish Eater's Club') formed in Paris. Bohemian members include the writers Gautier, Balzac and Baudelaire.

1850: United States census counts 8,327 hemp plantations (with a minimum size of 2,000 acres) growing cannabis hemp for industrial purposes.

1856: The British government begins to tax India's trade in ganja and charas.

1857: US writer and drug experimenter Fitzhugh Ludlow publishes *The Hasheesh Eater.*

1857: Smith Brothers of Edinburgh start to market a highly active extract of *Cannabis indica* in tinctures.

1868: The Emir of Egypt makes the possession of cannabis a capital offence.

1870: Worried about cannabis use among

ndian workers, South Africa bans the smoking,
se or possession of hemp by Indians.

876: At the Centennial Exposition in
'hiladelphia, visitors to the Turkish Hashish
.xposition toke up in order to 'enhance their fair
xperience'.

877: The Sultan of Turkey makes cannabis
legal.

883: Hashish-smoking parlours are open for
usiness in every major American city. Police
stimate there are 500 such parlours in New York
City alone.

890: Queen Victoria's personal physician, Sir
Russell Reynolds, prescribes cannabis for her
menstrual cramps.

890: The Greek Department of Interior
prohibits the import, cultivation and use of
ashish.

894–96: The seven volume report of the
ndian Hemp Drugs Commission concludes,
... regular, moderate use of ganja or bhang
produces the same effects as moderate and
egular doses of whisky'.

898: The Spanish-American War erupts.
During the war, the marijuana-smoking army of
Pancho Villa seizes 800,000 acres of Mexican

timberland belonging to newspaper magnate
William Randolph Hearst. The timber was used
to manufacture newsprint for Hearst's publishing
empire. Hearst begins a 30-year propaganda
campaign denouncing Spaniards, Mexican-
Americans and Latinos as lazy pot-smoking
layabouts.

1911: The white minority in South Africa
outlaws cannabis ingestion in an attempt to force
blacks to stop practising ancient Dagga religions.

1914: Congress passes the Harrison Narcotics
Act, its first attempt to control recreational use
of drugs.

1925: Concerned by the high number of 'goof
butts' being smoked by off-duty servicemen in
Panama, the US government sponsors the
Panama Canal Zone Report. The report
concludes that marijuana does not pose a
problem, and recommends that no criminal
penalties be applied to its use or sale.

1931: Treasury Secretary Andrew Mellon
appoints future nephew-in-law Harry J. Anslinger
to head the newly-formed Federal Bureau of
Narcotics.

1936–38: William Randolph Hearst's
newspaper empire fuels a tabloid journalism
propaganda campaign against marijuana.
Headlines such as 'Marihuana Makes Fiends of

Boys in 30 Days; Hashish Goads Users to Blood-Lust' create terror of the 'killer weed from Mexico'. Hearst is credited with bringing the word 'marijuana' into the English language. The Hearst papers also run racist articles about 'marijuana-crazed Negroes' raping white women and playing 'voodoo-satanic' jazz music.

14 April 1937: The Treasury Department secretly introduces its 'marijuana tax bill' through the House Ways and Means Committee, bypassing more appropriate venues.

Spring 1937: Congress holds hearings on the Marijuana Tax Act. Dr James Woodward, representing the American Medical Association, testifies that the law could deny the world a potential medicine. FBN commissioner Harry Anslinger and the Ways and Means Committee quickly denounce Woodward and the AMA.

December 1937: The Marijuana Tax Act is made Federal law, making cannabis illegal and annihilating the multi-billion dollar hemp industry.

1937–39: The Federal Bureau of Narcotics prosecutes 3,000 doctors for 'illegally' prescribing cannabis-derived medications. In 1939, the American Medical Association reaches an agreement with Harry Anslinger, and over the following decade only three doctors are prosecuted.

1941: *Popular Mechanics* introduces Henry Ford's plastic car, manufactured from and fuelled by cannabis. Hoping to free his company from the grasp of the petroleum industry, Ford illegally grew cannabis for years after the federal ban.

1942: Harry Anslinger is appointed to a top-secret committee charged with finding a 'truth serum' for the Office of Strategic Services (OSS) forerunner of the CIA. The group picks a form of hashish oil as their truth serum of choice, but abandon the idea in 1943.

1943–48: Harry Anslinger orders all Federal Bureau of Narcotics agents to conduct surveillance and keep files on marijuana 'crimes' by jazz and swing musicians. He envisions a nationwide bust of all pot-smoking musicians simultaneously. Under surveillance are Thelonius Monk, Louis Armstrong, Duke Ellington and Dizzy Gillespie among others. Anslinger's superior at the Treasury Department hears of the plan and writes to stop Anslinger: 'Mr Foley disapproves!'

1944: New York Mayor LaGuardia's Marijuana Commission concludes that there is no link between cannabis and violence, instead citing beneficial effects of marijuana. Harry Anslinger goes berserk, denouncing Mayor LaGuardia and threatening doctors with prison terms if they carry out independent research on cannabis.

1948: Anslinger now declares that using cannabis causes the user to become peaceful and pacifistic. He also claims that the Communists would use cannabis to weaken Americans' will to fight, a complete reversal of earlier testimony in 1937, when he told Congress that 'marijuana is the most violence-causing drug in the history of mankind'.

1951: According to United Nations estimates, there are approximately 200 million marijuana users in the world, the major centres being India, Egypt, North Africa, Mexico and the US.

1952: The first cannabis arrest in the UK is made at the Number 11 Club in Soho, London.

1961: UN Treaty 406 Single Convention on Narcotic Drugs seeks to outlaw cannabis use and cannabis cultivation worldwide, and to eradicate cannabis smoking entirely within 25–30 years.

1962: President John F. Kennedy forces Harry Anslinger into retirement. After his assassination in 1963, associates of Kennedy claimed that he used cannabis for back pain and planned to legalize marijuana during his second term.

1962: The first hashish (as opposed to kif) is made in Morocco.

1964: In the US, the first 'head shop' for the sale of cannabis-related goods is opened by the Thelin brothers in San Francisco.

1964: Cannabis' active ingredient, Tetrahydracannabinol, THC Delta-9 for short, is first isolated by Dr Raphael Mechoulam of the University of Tel Aviv.

1967: Keith Richard and Mick Jagger are busted at Richard's home for marijuana possession.

1967: The UK legalization campaign group SOMA publishes a petition in *The Times*; it urges legalization of cannabis. The Beatles and many well-known figures sign it. Some 3,000 people hold a 'smoke-in' in Hyde Park.

1967: Secretly funded by Jimi Hendrix, Abbie Hoffman and the Yippies mail out 3,000 joints to addresses chosen at random from the New York City phone book. They offer the recipients the chance to discover what all the fuss is about, but remind them that they are now criminals for possessing cannabis.

1968: In the UK, a Home Office select committee, chaired by Baroness Wootton, concludes that cannabis is no more harmful than tobacco or alcohol, and recommends that the penalties for all marijuana offences be reduced. It is immediately rejected by the Government.

1970: In Canada, the LeDain Report recommends the legalization of personal possession. It finds that cannabis use increases self-confidence, feelings of creativity and sensual

FAIR SMOKE	SMELL	TASTE	EFFECT	CANNABISCUP
Fair Smoke	Nice and spicy	Hazy	Very strong high	
Fair Smoke	Nice and spicy	Pepper, hazy	Very strong clear high	
Fair Smoke	Nice and spicy	Sweet and hazy	Very strong high	
Fair Smoke	Pungent	Sweet and sour	Heavy stoned, sit down	
	Sweet haze	Sweet , spicy	Strong high	2000
Fair Smoke	Fresh . sweet	Sweet	Stoned	1998
	Citrus	Sweet citrus	Strong stoned	
Fair Smoke	Like mango	Very fruity	Nice high	
Fair Smoke	Spicy,lemon	Citrus, spicy	Strong high	
Fair Smoke	Fruity	Sweet , fruity	Stoned	
Fair Smoke	Fruity	Full , fruity	Strong stoned	1995
Fair Smoke	Like fruity gum	Very fruity	Strong stoned	
	Spicy, lemon	Spicy	Very strong stoned	
Fair smoke	Fruity , fresh	Nice and sweet	Strong stoned	
	Spicy	Strong spicy	Stoned	1997
Fair Smoke	Pungent	Spicy	Strong high	
	Strong,spicy	Strong, full	Stoned	
Fair Smoke	Stong, spicy	Strong full	Stoned	
	Fruity	Full fruity	Mild stoned	
	Mixed	Mixed	Mild stoned	

FAIR SMOKE	SMELL	TASTE	EFFECT	CANNABISCUP
	Spicy	Spicy	High, Red eyes	
	Sour ,spicy	Spicy	High	
	Sweet,spicy	Sweet,sunshine	High	

FAIR SMOKE	SMELL	TASTE	EFFECT	CANNABISCUP
Fair smoke	Sweet ,flowers, full	Strong, rich	Psychedelic high	2001
Fair smoke	Sweet ,flowers, full	Strong, rich	Psychedelic high	2000
Fair smoke	Sweet ,full	Strong	Very high	
Fair smoke	Strong, flowers	Full, rich, unique	Heavy stoned	2002
Fair Smoke	Sweet, flowers	Spicy, little flat	Uplifting High	
Fair smoke	Deep ,full, spicy	Rich,clean	Very strong high	
	Full, spicy	Strong, earth	Strong high	1997
Fair Smoke	Sweet, full	Full, rich	Very strong stoned	
Fair Smoke	Clean real Afghani smell	Earth, sweet	Clear strong high	
Fair Smoke	Earth, sweet	Clean, real Nepalese smell	Clear strong high	
Fair smoke	Flowers	Sweet, rich	Strong high	
Fair smoke	Flowers	Sweet	High	
	Earth	Sweet	High	
	Strong	Strong, sweet	Stoned	
	Flowers	Strong, sweet	High	
	Real nepalese smell	Earth spicy	Highly recommended	

Wij streven naar langdurige relaties m...
bereid zijn alleen biologische bestrijd...
voeding te gebruiken. Wij adviseren d...
ontwikkeling van hun product . Deze
voldoen aan de door ons gestelde vo...
met controle op naleving van deze v...
hopen wij een evenwichtig assortime...
hoge kwaliteit samen te kunnen stell...
Alle Dampkring producten die voldoe...
voorwaarden kunt u herkennen aan

JOINTS

NAME	P...
Moonshine	
Tbizla	
Kali Mist (pure)	
Ak-47 (pure)	
White Widow	
AK-47	
Haze	
Maroc	
Marihuana	
Thai	
SIXPACKS	

SEEDS

NAME	
diesel	
Kali Mist	
AK-47	
Buddha's Sister	
Bubble Gum	
Nebula	
Sage	

SPECIAL OFFERS

NAME	

awareness, and reduces tension, hostility and aggression. The report recommends that possession laws be repealed.

1970: R. Keith Stroup founds the US-based National Organization for Reform of Marijuana Laws (NORML).

1971: The UK's Misuse of Drugs Act lists cannabis as a Class B drug (along with amphetamine and codeine) and bans its medical use. The Act prescribes a maximum five years' imprisonment for possession.

1972: In the Netherlands, the Baan Commission reports to the Dutch Minister of Health suggesting that cannabis trade below 0.25kg (8oz) should be considered as a misdemeanour only.

1973: The US Shafer Commission declares that personal use of marijuana should be decriminalized, as should casual distribution of small amounts for no or insignificant remuneration. President Nixon says, 'I am against legalizing marijuana.'

1973: Oregon becomes the first US state to take steps towards the legalization of cannabis. For the next 25 years, possession of 28g (1oz) of marijuana is considered the equivalent of a misdemeanour, with no criminal record.

1973: Nepal bans cannabis shops and export of charas (hand-rolled hash).

1973: The Afghan government makes hashish production and sales illegal.

1975: In the US, the FDA establishes a 'Compassionate Use' programme for medical marijuana.

1976: The Netherlands adopt a tolerant attitude to cannabis, and many coffee shops and youth centres are allowed to sell it *(see photo left)*.

1976: The Ford Administration bans research on the use of natural cannabis derivatives for medicine. Private pharmaceutical corporations are allowed to do limited 'no high' research.

1978: New Mexico becomes the first US state to make cannabis available for medical use.

1980: Paul McCartney spends 10 days in prison in Japan for the possession of cannabis.

1988: In Washington, DEA Judge Francis Young states that 'Marijuana in its natural form is one of the safest therapeutically active substances known to man'. He recommends that medical use of marijuana should be allowed for certain illnesses. The DEA rejects the ruling.

1989: A government-funded study at the St Louis Medical University determines that the human brain has receptor sites for THC to which no other known compounds will bind.

30 December 1989: Ignoring evidence to the contrary, DEA Director John Lawn orders that cannabis remain on the Schedule One narcotics list, reserved for drugs that have no known medical use.

1990: As the drug war gets uglier, 390,000 American citizens are arrested on marijuana-related charges.

5 September 1990: Los Angeles Police Chief Darryl Gates testifies before the US Senate Judiciary Committee that 'casual drug users should be taken out and shot'.

1992: The Frankfurt Charter is signed by 17 European cities agreeing to tolerate social use of cannabis.

1992: The UK government issues licences to grow cannabis for industrial uses or scientific research.

1995: The Henrion Commission Report supports decriminalization of cannabis and calls for a two-year trial period of regulated retail trade in cannabis. The French Government rejects these proposals.

1998: Italy and Belgium decriminalize cannabis, making it impossible to be prosecuted for possession for personal consumption. Italy permits small-scale cultivation of cannabis for own use.

1998: The British House of Lords rules that the Government should make cannabis available to the sick without further delay, but they are against legalization for recreational use. Jack Straw, Home Secretary, rejects the report.

2001: The British Government announces its intention to move cannabis from class B to class C, making possession a non-arrestable offence.

2004: The British Government downgrades cannabis from class B to class C.

Sources:
Jack Herer, *The Emperor Wears No Clothes*, 1994 edition
Jonathon Green, *Cannabis*, 2002 edition

Right: Every year on 1 May global demonstrations take place demanding the legalization of marijuana. This particular demo ended in Brockley Park in London and finished with... er... expected results.

"The importation and sale of marijuana is condemned and punished as a serious crime, but we accept as legitimate the manufacture and sale of an infinitely more addictive and deadly drug: the nicotine in cigarettes that cost the lives of 390,000 American citizens last year." *Jimmy Carter*

"I believe that God left certain plants upon our planet to help speed up and facilitate our evolution."

Bill Hicks

Cannabis FAQ

If you've got questions about the use of marijuana, from how to get high to the long-term effects, then we've got the answers...

Q: Is it addictive?

A: There is little evidence to suggest that cannabis itself is physically addictive. Some would argue that there is a risk of mental addiction, where the mind finds it very hard to go without getting high, but this is normally seen in people who use it on a very regular basis. However, tobacco is incredibly addictive, both physically and mentally, due to its nicotine content. As most people smoke cannabis mixed with tobacco, there is some danger that an addiction will occur. Try to smoke pure marijuana, or mix it with a herbal smoking mixture which doesn't contain nicotine.

Q: How much should I use in a spliff?

A: Generally you require very little good weed or hash to get high; just a thin layer in a spliff will normally do, and 3.5g (1/8oz) will generally be

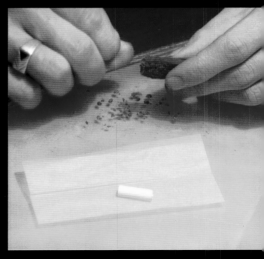

Above: Skinning up takes skill and patience, so keep practising. Once you've cracked it you'll be everybody's mate.

enough for 10–15 joints. However, as the strength depends on the THC content, you will find you need to use more weed with a low THC content to get stoned. Be careful: some hydroponic strains are incredibly potent. One way to judge the potency before smoking (although it's not 100 per cent reliable) is to look for the amount of white THC crystals covering the weed – the more there are, the stronger it will be. A strong smell is not always a good indication of actual strength.

Q: What are the health risks?

A: Because of its illegal status, research into the health risks associated with cannabis is not as comprehensive as it should be. However, we know that smoking is bad, whatever you smoke, because it exposes your body to more than average levels of carcinogens and free radicals. Current medical thinking would suggest that smoking three pure joints a day is equivalent to 20 cigarettes, but this has been disputed, and light-to-moderate users are less likely to suffer than cigarette smokers. On the other hand, its stress-busting qualities are thought to be very beneficial to our well-being.

Q: What are the best ways to smoke it?

A: Most of the harmful byproducts of cannabis are released when it is burned, but many more can be filtered out with the use of a water bong. Smoking it pure (through a pipe or chillum) or with a herbal smoking mixture is far better than mixing it with tobacco (and the high is much cleaner and more intense). Possibly the best way to 'smoke' it is by using a vaporizer, which heats up the cannabis until the active ingredient is vaporized for inhaling, but the plant material around it remains unburned and therefore the nasty chemicals are not released.

Q: Does eating it have a different effect?

A: Very much so. A good hash brownie is enough to reduce even the most hardened of smokers to a giggling wreck. One of the most common mistakes made when eating cannabis is not having the patience to let the high come on. When smoking, the THC can get working straight away, as the lungs offer it quick passage into the blood stream and to the brain. When you eat cannabis, it has to be digested before it has an effect, so leave it a couple of hours before you decide whether to have another brownie or not.

Q: Can I be arrested for possession?

A: This depends where you are in the world. Most European countries are now tolerant to small amounts for personal use, but it is always best to check – even a small amount can land you in jail in Greece. The US is so fanatical about its drugs war that it would be foolish not to be incredibly careful about carrying the drug.

For more information about legality around the world, check out the Cannabis Campaigners Guide at www.ccguide.org.uk.

Q: Am I allowed to grow marijuana?

A: This is probably the most clouded issue in the whole cannabis debate, made more so by the availability of seeds on the Internet and on sale in head shops. Officially, in the UK at least, you still need a license from the Home Office before you grow plants, and unless you are a big medical company doing research, the chances of being granted one are pretty slim.

Q: Is cannabis just for getting high?

A: When you get stoned for the first time, the effect may seem to be unmanageable and counterproductive to anything you want to do. However, regular users can manage this effect and find that the mind-freeing result of cannabis is excellent for meditation, lateral thinking and creative pursuits where the mind benefits from being less anchored.

Left: Even if the laws where you live are relaxed – see this toker in Brixton, London – it still pays to be a bit more discrete! Even if the police do nothing, some members of the public have a less understanding or tolerant approach to cannabis.

Although its medical uses are slowly being investigated, there can be no doubt that it has an effect on a range of conditions from pain relief to increased mobility in MS sufferers.

The plant also makes excellent rope, paper and cloth, to mention just a few of its additional uses.

Q: Will it affect my fertility?

A: Research in the US and Ireland suggests that heavy use makes sperm behave erratically, using up too much energy before reaching the egg and, more crucially, unable to digest the egg's outer layer when it gets there. However, research in this area is still limited, and certainly many marijuana smokers throughout history have had no problems fathering children.

Q: What should I expect when I first take it?

A: The effects you can expect are usually (in order): a slight tingling of the feet, numbness of extremities, an inability to stop smiling and giggling, an added dimension to colours, sound, smells and other senses, a feeling of being separate from events around you, the munchies and, finally, tiredness. This is only a rough guide, though, and not everyone experiences it this way. Non-smokers who smoke a joint for the first time tend to find the event a bit of a letdown because they either don't take the smoke into the lungs, or spend much of the time coughing.

Bibliography

Barret, Leonard E Senior: *The Rastafarians*, Boston, Beacon Press, 1997

Boon, Marcus: *The Road Of Excess*, Harvard University Press, 2002

Clarke, Robert C: *Hashish!*, Red Eye Press, California,1998

Davenport-Hines, Richard: *The Pursuit of Oblivion*, London, Weidenfeld & Nicolson, 2000

Frank, Mel: *Marijuana Grower's Inside Guide*, California, Red Eye Press, 1988

Green, Jonathon: *Cannabis*, London, Pavilion, 2002

Herer, Jack: *The Emperor Wears No Clothes*, Quick American Archives, 1979

Jones, Nick: *Spliffs* London, Chrysalis Books, 2003

King, Jason: *The Cannabible*, California, Ten Speed Press, 2001

Ludlow, Fitzhugh: *The Hasheesh Eater*, New York, Harper and Brothers, 1857

Marks, Howard: *Mr Nice*, London, Secker & Warburg, 1996

Marks, Howard: *The Howard Marks Book of Dope Stories*, London, Vintage, 2001

Matthews, Patrick: *Cannabis Culture*, London, Bloomsbury, 1999

Mezzrow, Milton & Wolfe Bernard: *Really The Blues*, New York, Random House, 1946

Preston, Brian: *Pot Planet: Adventures in Global Marijuana Culture*, Grove Press, 2002

Rosenthal, Ed: *Marijuana Growers Handbook*, California, Quick American Publishing Company, 1984

Shapiro, Harry: *Waiting For The Man*, London, Mandarin, 1990

Sloman, Larry: *Reefer Madness: The History of Marijuana in America*, New York, Bobbs-Merrill, 1979

Solomon, David: *The Marihuana Papers*, New York, Bobbs-Merrill, 1966

Watts, Alan W: *The Joyous Cosmology*, New York, Random House, 1965

Acknowledgements

Author's note

The Author would like to thank the many unsung heroes who made this book possible. To Rob Tribe and Michelle Guilford for their very excellent writing skills and sensimilla savvy. To the unbelievably helpful Mark Evans at Everybodydoesit.com for letting us raid his unbelievably huge database of images. Unbelievable. A quick hullo to Dez Skinn for lending me his comics and advice, and a big thanks out to Nick Jones, without whom this book would not have been possible. The biggest shout goes out to David and Julie Pilcher, Adele King and Megan and Oskar Pilcher-King – the five most important people in my life. I love you all very much. This one's also for Rita and Enzo, the two biggest stoners I know! Happy tokin'!